Sailing the Waterways
of Russia's North

Sailing the Waterways of Russia's North

Irene Campbell-Grin

SELF
PUBLISHING
HOUSE

Publishing services provided by Self Publishing House

All photographs by Irene Campbell-Grin
except p125 by Elsbeth Vankerk on *Spirit of Aeolus*,
used with permission

Editor & designer: Rachel Atkins

Paperback ISBN 978–1–9163873–1–7
eBook ISBN 978–1–9163873–2–4

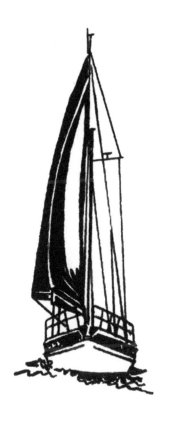

Fereale
which means *in love*
in the Old Frisian language

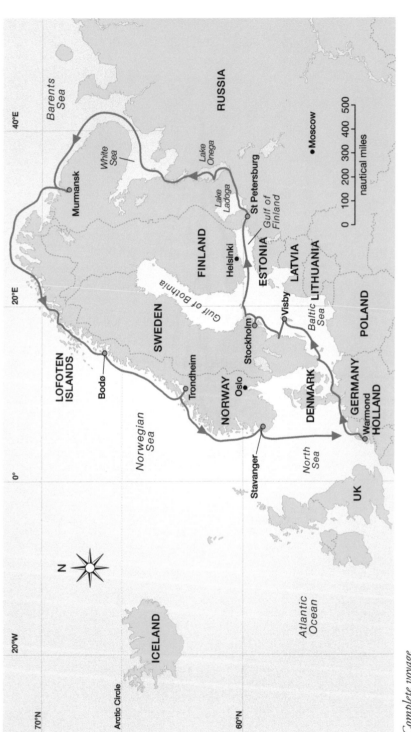

Complete voyage

St.Petersburg City Administration

St.Petersburg Sailing Union

1703-2003
The 300th anniversary of
St.Petersburg

Invitation to St.Petersburg

January 31, 2000

Dear Ladies and Gentlemen!
Dear sailing friends!

Government of St.Petersburg, St.Petersburg Sailing Union, marine authorities, citizens and yachtsmen have the great honour to invite the yachting fleet of participants of the Baltic Millennium Rally, organized by the Cruising Association to visit St.Petersburg in summer 2000 to celebrate millennium together with russian sailing collegues.

The whole history of Russia as a great marine state is connected with St.Petersburg. The creation of the shipbuilding industry, construction of the largest in Russia sea port, formation of marine and shipbuilding science and education, the brightest victories of the Russian Navy - all these highlights of the marine history of Russia are connected with our city.

We will be happy to show our guests the amazing architecture of St.Petersburg, to acquaint them with the history of its past and present culture. Hundreds of museums, scores of theaters, palaces, unique in their beaty and grace, are waiting for you.

Yachting tourism and boating are not so popular in St.Petersburg and in Russia as in European countries. But we understand how important it will become in future for the social life of our city. We are very thankful to all participants and the Baltic Millennium Rally Planning Group for tremendous efforts to arrange this long distance Rally via Baltic Sea to St.Petersburg and via inland waterways to Petrozavodsk in Karelia and further to the White Sea.

We will do all our best to prepare in proper way the marina facilities in St.Petersburg for the fleet of Baltic Millenium Rally, to assist in your cultural programme and we will support you in the arrangements for sailing via Russian inland waterways.

From the bottom of my heart I wish the organizers big success and all participants fair winds on their way to Russia and via Russia.

I am sure that your visit to St.Petersburg and Russia in 2000 will not be the last and you will join us in the celebrations of the 300-th anniversaries of St.Petersburg and Petrozavodsk in summer 2003.

**Welcome to St.Petersburg, the city of white nights,
the marine capital of Russia.**

Vice-governor of St.Petersburg,
President of St.Petersburg
Sailing Union

Vladimir Grishanov

Gordon & Irene

Contents

Preface

The reason for writing this log was driven by my desire to put our experiences on paper and for our love of the sea, which we share.

I am writing in my second language because neither my husband, Gordon, nor our children, Inge and Saskia, are fluent in Dutch. It is the only way for me to share my inner feelings with them and ensure they won't stay on the shelf unread.

I would like to dedicate this log to my husband who had the courage to make the most difficult decision of all: to give up his job in the hope of getting it back at the end of our five months' travel, something one cannot take for granted. Not once did I lose my faith in him to somehow find a solution to the problems we experienced on our way. I have always known that we would come back safely. Also my dedication is extended to members of our family, especially my dear mother. She, like many others, did everything in her power to make sure that nothing stood in our way; and to Inge and Saskia, without whose undying trust we would not have gone.

Last but not least I would like to thank the Cruising Association for having organised the rally. Without them this story would not have happened.

Introduction

A year has gone by since we heard from the Cruising Association (CA) that they were planning a trip to Russia, a voyage through the country's inland waterways to the White Sea, Barents Sea, North Cape and back via the west coast of Norway. For years we have been dreaming of sailing to exciting places, and ever since we had a six-year spell in Oslo back in the seventies we have longed to return to Norway. But, however confident we feel about our ability at sea, and that of our boat, we never would have had the courage to tackle Russia alone, especially well beyond St Petersburg. This was the perfect opportunity to put words into action and turn our dreams into reality. On hearing about the CA's Blue Onega Rally, we knew instantly that this was the one for us.

At last there was a real purpose in our lives again; to use our beloved *Fereale* for the reason she was built. A strong, twelve-metre sailing boat—with bilge keels, cutter rigged and made of steel—a 'one off'. She was built for the owner of a well-known boat yard in Friesland some twenty years ago, and he put all his love into her. She is an indestructible boat, and one Gordon and I fell in love with at first sight some five years ago. Since then *Fereale* has become part of us as we have lived on her ever since. Down below there is an engine room with standing headroom, a workbench, watertight doors and much more. We never tire of her beautiful teak interior, and we give her all the love and care that she needs. Every ache or pain, however big or small, is seen to, for which she rewards us in return. To me she is a whale inside which we live to keep her breathing.

Fereale

All through the year we have planned and looked forward to every bit of information coming our way; briefing and pilotage notes, customs and immigration requirements, chart planning and other useful references. Notes put together by CA members and Honorary Local Representatives (HLRs) in each Baltic state have formed a rally guide, which reads more like a Baltic pilot book; information to which any member of the Cruising Association has access. We also received encouraging letters from Vladimir Ivankiv, the Cruising Association's HLR in St Petersburg, who proved to be an invaluable link.

During the year I went on navigation and radio communication courses and taught myself how to play the concertina, in between running errands for Gordon on my moped. We cannot waste our precious time at weekends, as they are the only days we have available to work on *Fereale*.

We need to leave Warmond on May 1st in order to be able to meet up with the rest of the fleet in Den Helder on the 8th. There we will meet the other boats, all of them leaving at different stages. About thirty-two will go anti-clockwise around the Baltic, ten as far as Petrozavodsk, of which five, including *Fereale*, will go all the way around the top.

Preparations for a trip like this can go on forever with the risk of never going. There comes a time when you have to trust the fact that you have done enough. We have a few days left to do the last finishing touches. The pump, valves and hoses for the foul water tank still have to be installed; not an easy task with Gordon still working full time and coming home tired in the evenings. But soon it will be time to pick the fruits of our labour.

Not until Den Helder will our excess baggage leave the boat. Dear Mum, willing as always to help us in every way, will find a place for it somewhere in her house. It will not be the first time she has helped us in this way. We need to make room for our daughter, Inge, and her husband, Richard, who will be joining us in St Petersburg. Later, not until Petrozavodsk, will Gordon's brother, Colin, be joining us as far as Murmansk.

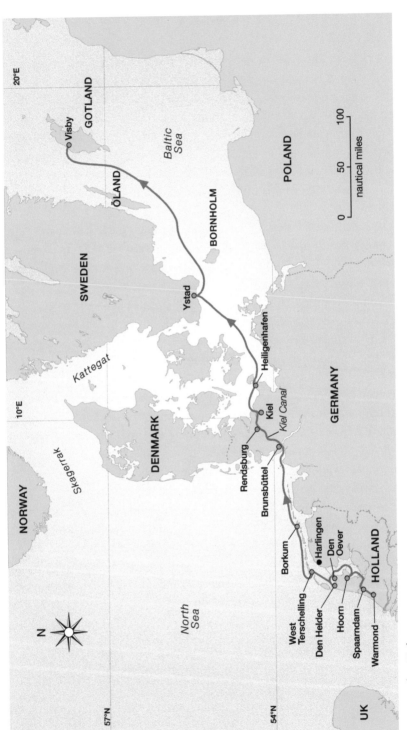

Warmond to Visby

Casting Off

24th April, 2000
Seven days to go.

The cards are pouring in, wishing us fair winds. The sun is shining and inside *Fereale* it is hot. The saloon table and floor are covered in paperwork. A last-minute sort out, to hand over our administration to Inge when we see her in Den Helder. Gordon is fitting three brand-new, self-tailing winches on the mast; a must, if I am to be able to handle the sails as well as him. Our harbour has suddenly come to life as Holland slowly wakes up from her winter sleep.

One more week to go, and the clock is ticking.

30th April, 2000
Last night, the owner of the yard and his wife came round for a drink. Bending over our enormous world atlas, we were finally able to show them the reason for all our hard work. With Jan and Paddy, on a neighbouring boat, we finished a bottle of champagne, and my friend, Hanneke, dropped by, and Joke, so dear and loyal. She was the first one to know about our plans and has watched them grow since birth.

1st May, 2000
On our way at last. It is 5am. Emotionally I turned around as we left our harbour and waved, but to nobody. It is early after all. My mind is going round in circles. Unable to keep the tears away, and for no reason at all I did not just cry, but sobbed. We found a nice little note stuck to the boat this morning

from Jan and Paddy, they must have come round after we had gone to bed. With glee on his face Gordon is rapidly getting used to the idea of not having to work for the next five months.

Arrived at De Rietpol at last, a tiny harbour in Spaarndam, just outside Haarlem, with enough time in hand to buy and replace one more winch. Pleased as punch we bought the only one left in the shop and started walking back towards the boat. Then an outcry, as the gate slammed shut on Gordon's fingers. With the old winch still in one hand, we watched the new one disappear into the water. "Damn," he said whilst changing into his swimming trunks and goggles. No huge splash as he lowered himself gently into the icy cold water, triumphantly holding up the new winch like a trophy a few minutes later.

2nd May, 2000

By midday we had already carried out our second rescue mission. Was this a taste of things to come? A huge wooden boeier from Warmond beckoned for our help, as they lay tied to a post. "Problems with our engine," they shouted, "we've mixed diesel and water. Can you give us a tow?" What fools, we thought, but being good citizens we towed them to the nearest harbour. We should not have been so quick to judge, as we discovered later during our travels, when we proved to be such fools ourselves.

With gale-force winds on the nose we headed for the IJsselmeer, rather than the North Sea. At least there we don't have to contend with the tide as well as the wind. I am feeling seasick, and both of us still have to get into the swing of things. Annoying little things to solve like the VHF radio in the cockpit, which has given up the ghost. The weather is horrible, with a strong headwind, and we are motoring to make progress with the seagulls following in our wake. We have also been trying out our radar, still a novelty to us. In the lee of the land the harbour of Hoorn felt sheltered with a berth, ready and waiting.

3rd May, 2000

Nearly 9pm and our technician who fixed the VHF has just left. He soldered a loose connection for us in his workshop, managing to fit us into his busy schedule. Even better was the news that the bill would go to the manufacturers. The rest of Gordon's time was spent struggling with a leaking, smelly toilet. He came to the conclusion that working in the office was more relaxing; working on the boat was tiring and sailing exhausting. The things you say when you are tired... Relaxing over a few drinks in a pub soon sorted that one out!

4th May, 2000

Mum calls as often as she can, and so do the girls, all of them making the most of us still being within range. Gordon, following his dive in the icy cold water, has a shocking cold, though still preferable, he says, to repairing smelly toilets! It is 5pm and we are on our way to Den Oever. I must say, we do work hard for our living and will sleep well when we finally get there tonight.

We did not arrive until nine o'clock in the evening after the most intensive navigation ever, and this is only the IJsselmeer! Dense fog closed in on us, and our radar was fully christened. Silly perhaps, but after safely mooring up we congratulated each other on our safe arrival. Another five thousand nautical miles to go and we call this tough? We shall have to look at it as a good test for things to come.

5th May, 2000

At last we are in the Waddenzee. It is a good thing to get out to sea whilst the locks are still half empty, before the mad rush of the Dutch summertime. The fog has cleared, and the weather is beautiful. It has taken us a little while but at last we feel in the right mood. Gently we thread our way through the sandbanks and see Texel in the distance. The channels we go through are like wide roads, and we need to keep well to starboard. Time to tidy up down below and do my spin-drying!

We arrived in Den Helder at about 1pm and soon recognised the participating boats by their rally flags. We had met most of the skippers and crew before, at a convention in Reading, and it did not take us long before we were invited on board *Reflections* for a welcome drink.

6th May, 2000

Up early, as we need to prepare for the arrival of my dear friend, Winny, and her husband, Bert. Whilst Winny and I chatted and soaked up the rays of the sun on our aft deck, Gordon showed Bert our intended route. Our children and son-in-law, Richard, are arriving from England tonight, and my entire Dutch family tomorrow. Gordon helped Willem, the skipper of one of the

Farewell party at Den Helder

boats joining us around the North Cape, with something that needed muscle. Like this, everyone in the fleet is busy doing something. All the boats are so different in shape and size, and with great interest I walked about and talked to skippers and crew. Then, a tap on my shoulder and there were Inge, Richard, Saskia and my sister, Marijse; they had arrived earlier than expected, laden with goodies. We enjoyed a few hours together before they had to rush off to Mum, who was expecting them for dinner.

7th May, 2000
Today is the day eleven members of our family will be visiting us. It could not be a nicer day, with the sun high in the sky, which means that we can all be up on deck, rather than squeezed inside *Fereale's* belly. They told us to be lazy, and that they would bring all the food. When they arrived, the harbour looked a wonderful sight with all the boats dressed overall. We ate, drank and sang songs, and Steven, my cousin, even climbed the mast to take some pictures. We were showered with love, gifts, and cards. In the meantime, more and more boats have arrived carrying the rally flag. After we said goodbye it was time to reflect on our special day and how lucky we are in having such wonderful children and family. I was unable to sleep that night.

8th May, 2000
Today is our departure day and official rally start, with Terschelling our next port of call. The route takes us via the Waddenzee, quite an experience with those fierce tides! Tomorrow we shall go around the outside to Borkum, to avoid all the zigzagging between the sandbanks.

9th May, 2000
The sunrise is lovely and we are on our way. It is 5am and the seals with their comical heads greet us, as if to say 'good morning' or 'goodbye' perhaps. Gordon has gone back to his bunk and is having a well-deserved rest, whilst *Fereale* and I struggle to pass Terschelling with the wind dead on the nose. It is a shame that we did not get time to explore Terschelling last night, but unfortunately this will be the case in many of the ports, owing to our hectic schedule.

During the course of the day I also managed to catch up on some much-needed sleep. It is foggy, and our radar did not detect a fibreglass boat near us. Gordon noticed that they were carrying one of those modern spiral radar reflectors. Poor chap, he thinks every ship will see him but they won't. By the time we reach Borkum tonight we will have been on the go for seventeen hours. Slowly we are getting into the watch-keeping routine. It is 7pm and Borkum is to port of us. Even with the island so close we won't have reached the harbour entrance before ten tonight. Having first gone aground at the entrance of Baalmann yacht harbour, we finally moored up in the Burkana harbour. It seems that all the boats aiming for Borkum went aground in the same place.

10th May, 2000
Borkum is an old-fashioned harbour with huge wooden pontoons that move up and down with the tide. I feel very tired but shall have to get used to this way of living. Our harbour master is a tiny chap with a huge beard, who wears a knitted hat with a bobble on the top. He speaks every language under the sun and could not be more helpful. We took out our bikes and cycled the three miles into town, to shop and enjoy a coffee on the way, overlooking the sea. In the evening, all on board *Spirit of Aeolus*, *Du Bleiz*, *Avola*, *Reflections*, and *Fereale* get together. I wonder sometimes, with all this socialising, how we will all find the time and energy to plan the next leg.

11th May, 2000
Up early, to prepare the boat and ourselves for another sea passage. There is always something quite exiting about that. During the night another two boats arrived, they must be disappointed to see all of us leave so soon. Coastal sailing is strenuous, and we will be pleased to be out of tidal waters and into the Baltic. We heard that the boat *Brough Sands* has had to pull out of the rally, owing to engine problems. We feel very sorry for them, as we all know the hard work that goes into the planning of such a trip.

We are in two minds whether or not to stop at Helgoland. The wind is coming from the right direction, but it will mean arriving there at 2am. In a few hours' time we will pass the German island of Juist, our course is perfect and we are settling in nicely. Making coffee was a challenge, with the cooker swinging and the coffee pot in its clamps. Now that *Brough Sands* has pulled out, we are the only boat taking the northern route, via Sweden and Finland.

We don't mind at all, as we can go at our own pace.

Gordon looks snug on the saloon bunk covered by a duvet; I am busy plotting and spotting. When it was my time to rest, I tried sleeping in the fo'c's'le as the passage berth was littered with charts, but that was a big mistake! Time and time again I was thrown into the air and, feeling too sick to find anywhere more comfortable, I found myself back in the cockpit recovering. Gordon quickly sorted out the passage bunk for me but, seeing I was too ill to make use of it, he grabbed his chance for another rest.

I think about our children and my family and wish I had time to write. But there is far less chance of that than I had hoped. All I can do is scribble on this illegible pad from time to time. It is 8pm and I have still not managed to rest because I am feeling seasick. There are a lot of fishing boats about and it will soon be dark. To starboard of us, in the distance, is Langeoog Island. The decision was made to sail through the night, all the way to Brunsbüttel, where we should arrive in the morning. There is a huge swell and the wind is strong. We wonder what the other boats have done.

In the Elbe the seas were boiling, with wind over tide and a north-easterly force seven. The Elbe is notorious for its strong currents. Fortunately, the wind has been blowing from the north-east, but with wind over tide in a strong north-westerly, the seas can easily turn a ten-metre boat end over end. We are on our last leg now and have another hour to go till Brunsbüttel, then peace and sleep. What a night it has been, with only one hour's rest for me, and three for Gordon. It is definitely white-knuckle stuff out there. Who would want to go to Alton Towers, when one can go to the Elbe! I pity the boats behind us as I expect we will be one of the first to arrive in Brunsbüttel. *Fereale* deserves a bucket of fresh water and a bag of oats after this. To cap it all I strained a muscle in my right arm dealing with ropes in the locks and now it is in a sling.

13th May, 2000
Well rested and having used ice packs on my shoulder all night, I feel a lot better. We decided not to wait for the other boats, but to move on and stop somewhere along the Kiel Canal. No more locks for a while, we motor gently, in brilliant sunshine, up the Kiel Canal, occasionally meeting huge ships going the other way. Ships we have to avoid at sea now come within a few yards of us. My hand-washing routine works well as every day I soak our clothes in a

couple of plastic Tupperware buckets with lids and do the rinsing when I have water available ashore. I am still unable to lift my arm, but it is better than yesterday, which means there is improvement. The icepacks work well, and give icy comfort!

We have now reached the suburbs of Rendsburg and it all looks very prosperous, with the scenery so fresh at this time of the year. Some sinister-looking warships pass us and we wonder what weapons they carry. Diverting into the River Eider, we find a delightful yacht harbour in Büdelsdorf. The only thing you can hear is the sound of birds. What a difference after Brunsbüttel.

14th May, 2000
Just when we were about to leave, we were informed that not all the locks would open on a Sunday. Rightly or wrongly, we decided to stay another day and explore the area on our bikes. *Nefertiti*, some eighteen metres in length—the biggest boat in the fleet, soon joined us on our pontoon. Built entirely out of wood, she is a sheer delight down below. David and her crew have sailed her around the world, and entertained us with many tales over a bottle of wine, one of the several hundred he carried on board.

The Baltic

15th May, 2000

Off to Holtenau, where, once through the locks, we hoisted sail to Düsternbrook. The sail training ships in the area, bright blue water, wooded banks and holiday homes made a lovely sight. Such a different view from what we had seen before. We blessed our sunshade, as it was hot, and in the harbours hotter still. In Düsternbrook we were welcomed by four of the boats from our fleet, a number that soon increased to nine.

16th May, 2000

The best part of the day is always early in the morning when everyone is still sleeping. *Fereale* has had her first fresh water scrub since we left Holland; not everywhere is one allowed to use the water for that purpose. It feels very Scandinavian here already, with showers that consist of one huge room instead of individual cabins. A Canadian couple next to us, who are also in the rally, are still recovering from their North Sea experience. "It was ten times worse than crossing the Atlantic," they said. The crew from an English boat told us that they never wanted to see the Dutch coast again as they found it utterly boring. One more day in harbour and then we will part company with the others. The arrangement is that we email *Reflections* from time to time, to let them know of our whereabouts. The day was spent food shopping, resting, cycling and buying charts, with a party in the evening on *Spirit of Aeolus* held in our honour. From now we are on our own and won't meet up with the others till St Petersburg. A strange thought, but also quite a nice one. Though, as it turned out, we did sail together for one more day.

17th May, 2000
Early in the morning is the time for me to write my diary, and the time for me to reflect and have some peace and quiet. It is raining slightly, but that only clears the air. Although all the socialising is a bit much at times, we shall miss the company of our friends. Our VHF has given up the ghost and is able to receive but not transmit. This is a great shame as once on our way we noticed *Bathsheba* heading into a firing range area. I tried to call them up, but our VHF showed antenna failure. Without being able to warn them, we had to look on as they were intercepted by the navy and pointed in the right direction. We arrived in Heiligenhafen at about 5pm in bad weather, and were helped with our lines by the others. Gordon managed to do a temporary repair to the VHF, but needs to do a soldering job when the weather improves. With that we decided to stay in harbour one more day.

18th May, 2000
With the rally boats leaving around us we feel unsettled and also want to be on the move. Because of our delay we will probably sail through the night tomorrow as we still have a long way to go to St Petersburg. Willem, Elsbeth and crew kindly came round last night wishing us well, together with many others. With all this socialising we are not as organised as we would like to be, and things that need doing get put aside. We should prepare for tomorrow's long trek to Sweden, for instance, but we are having a good time and would not like to miss any of it.

19th May, 2000
Both of us feel apprehensive this morning. This often happens at the beginning of a journey into the unknown. It has to do with all the preparations that always have to take place. The wind is from the south-east, which is just right, and we are planning to sail through the night to Ystad in Sweden. If the wind stays this favourable we might sail through a second night too. All sails are up and we are doing five knots. It is 1pm and Gordon has gone down till the next waypoint in about two hours' time. We have to stay clear of a submarine exercise area, and I am kept very busy updating the log and plotting positions. The wind is

doing funny things, and I am pleased that Gordon is sleeping well as he needs a good rest. Me, I am happy as we are sailing a correct course according to the chart. I did have to get used to the idea of being on our own and not with the fleet anymore, but a positive point is that there is no more competitiveness, like who gets there first and at what time and speed. From now on we do our own thing, as *Fereale* is not a racer! Now and again, when Gordon has a waking spell, he knocks on the inside of the cockpit by his bunk. He worries when it gets a bit quiet, and checks to see that I have not fallen overboard. I do the same to him. It is inconsiderate of the navy to have these submarine exercise areas, as otherwise we would not have to make such detours all the time!

We have just had to avoid a pipe-laying vessel, and saw on the Navtex that it was called Sea Spider. Gordon called them up and asked if it was OK to pass to the south, which it was. We need to be on the ball all the time. On our port side in the distance is the Danish peninsula called Falster. Soon it will be dark and with a good dinner inside us we are ready for a long night. I am sitting on the aft hatch all dressed up in long johns, jeans, offshore jacket and hat, warm gloves, and have binoculars around my neck. We are just to port of the busy shipping lanes. Our course steers us clear of them, thank goodness. Nevertheless, there are annoying little posts sticking out of the water with tiny black flags on top. They are there to mark the nets of fishermen, but are never lit and are difficult to spot in the dark. It is important to see these little devils before *Fereale* gets a net stuck around the prop of her engine. At the moment we are still flying the Danish courtesy flag, but by morning it will be the Swedish one.

20th May, 2000
I have rested well, and it is 5am. Ystad in Sweden is another twenty-five miles away. Unfortunately, though, the sea has become dead calm and motor sailing is in order. Slowly we are getting the hang of how to use our new GMDSS radio, and it all seems less daunting than at first.

Ystad is a convenient and interesting staging post. It has a small well-kept marina with lots of facilities. This is where, for the first time ever, we saw a harbour master on roller skates! After catching up on lost sleep, we went out on our bikes to explore the area. What makes life so interesting is meeting the locals. The man on the boat next to us is an author, whose plan is to sail through Russia this very summer and out into the Black Sea. So far he has been unable to get a visa, he told us. Overnight I let him read one of the books from our library called *Sailing Round Russia*, written by Wallace Clark. Wallace is the father of Miles Clark who, in 1992, was the first person to circumnavigate both Russia and the Continent of Europe in his yacht *Wild Goose*. Sadly Miles died before the return journey to Ireland could be completed. Wallace, who had helped sail the first and last legs of the journey, wrote the book from extracts of Miles' log. I was also able to give our friend the address of Vladimir Ivankiv, the Honorary Local Representative of the CA in St Petersburg.

Our plan is to depart for Gotland tomorrow, another two nights at sea.

21st May, 2000

It is very peaceful early in the morning. There is hardly any wind and both of us are wondering if the rest of the fleet has arrived in Poland by now. A strange thought! We are on our way once more and slowly we skim past the most southern tip of Sweden. The coastline is gentle with sandy beaches, rounded green and black cliffs and cotton-wool clouds. The Baltic Sea is a kind sea unlike the North Sea; we know it will not always be like this. Gordon, having done his homework, has just beaten me to being the first one to hit the bunk. Our first waypoint is seven miles away, after which the GPS will tell me to steer a different course. In the various harbours *Fereale* gets lots of attention, as people wonder what type of boat she is. We can never give them a satisfying answer, as there is only one *Fereale*.

The weather is just right to try out our new spinnaker. With a sail area of ninety-four square metres, we watch excitedly as our speed doubles. As is usually the case, the wind increased in strength the moment it was aloft, and both of us are feeling apprehensive. To calm our nerves I made a strong cup of tea. What one must *not* do in such situations is fall overboard, and we have discussed what to do should this happen. No shipping lanes to worry about for a while, anyway, we should be clearly visible. A little while ago a light aircraft circled us twice, most likely the coastguard checking us out. Overland there are dubious-looking skies and we can hear thunder, a clear warning that it is time to take down our spinnaker. We are certainly being kept on our toes. Roll on Gotland.

22nd May, 2000

Morning has broken and we are passing Öland to port of us. There is precious little wind, it has been an easy night and with the engine on we are slowly motor sailing towards our goal. Perhaps I should whistle for the wind, as we could do with a little more, but I need to restrain myself from doing so.

The first time I heard someone whistle for the wind was in Indonesia, where we lived for two and a half years. A local chap took us sailing once in his fishing boat, a boat no wider than our behinds. With not enough wind to fill the sails he started to whistle. When I remarked to Gordon what a nice jolly chap he was, he told me that our little skipper was whistling for the wind. Suddenly the wind filled the sails to such strength that we had to hurry back to the beach. It was an amazing experience.

In 1989 we bought *Nusa Ina*, a Jakarta registered old fibreglass Folkboat derivative, a Bianca 27. It proved to be the best thing we ever did, and the only refuge from the teeming third world city of Jakarta. Whenever there was a decent moon we used to sail to the Thousand Islands on a Friday night after work, usually in the company of one or two other boats. We would arrive at the islands at about breakfast time the following day, sleep a little, and socialise with our children, their teenage friends and other adults under the coconut palms. How we ever had the courage to swim I will never know, but we did as long as someone was keeping a shark watch. *Nusa Ina* once had such a visitor, a harmless whale shark, but larger than the boat itself. After breakfast on Sunday, the boats would head back to Jakarta's main harbour, Tanjung Priok, where we usually arrived in the early evening.

However, during the Gulf War in 1991 there was a change in atmosphere in the country. All of a sudden the poorest of the poor were able to afford large transistor radios, and everyone in the street was listening to reports coming from Iraq. Saddam Hussein was highly praised, and President Bush was bad. Suddenly every white man, whatever his or her nationality, became a much-hated American in the eyes of the Indonesians. A real threat, a threat of the unknown, was hanging over us. When the American company Gordon was working for at the time put in an emergency evacuation plan for their staff, we decided to set about making a plan of our own. A plan to sail away if need be, to Australia or Hindu Bali. Easier than trying to bribe your way to the airport, where only the richest of the rich would succeed in getting a flight.

Following the company's plans never entered our minds. I remember trying to get to the Australian embassy in the much-troubled Jakarta at the time, where I managed to get visas for our family. To my utter surprise I found out that the Dutch embassy was prepared to evacuate us all, but that the British embassy would only help its own nationals. Our plan had to be a secret one, and from then on we decided that every Saturday Gordon would work on the upkeep of *Nusa Ina*, the first job being the strengthening of the deck underneath the mast step. In the meantime I secretly stocked up with water, money, food, fishing tackle and an enormous coconut knife. The chance of being marooned on a lonely island with a single coconut palm tree was a real one! Even a last minute shopping list was prepared for hitting the market on our way to Tanjung Priok. We had calculated that if things came to a head, all of us could have been at sea within the hour. In a way we were quite disappointed when our sail to Australia did not materialise, as all of us had been quite prepared to leave anything materialistic behind. But it is time to get back to the reality of now, and stop dreaming of the past.

If we continue at this speed we should arrive in Gotland by 2am and be able to rest and enjoy a full day. It is quite hypnotic watching the waves go past us faster than we are travelling. Real nail-biting stuff, this, as the next time we hoisted our spinnaker everything went horribly wrong. First it went up on the wrong forestay, next it wrapped itself around the radar scanner and remote compass, which compensates for our steel hull. Struggling so hard makes our learning curve a fast one. Our biggest mistake has been to position our radar scanner on the mast, instead of supporting it on a post from the aft deck. Both will have to be moved at some point. I am going down for a rest now, fully clothed in case there is a problem on deck.

After only one hour down, ominous clouds and thunder moved our way and it took all of ten minutes to take the whole lot down again. The air force is practising very low above the water, and I was woken up by what sounded like a huge whining sound all along the side of the boat. Strange for this non-aligned country to have gunboats and fighter planes all over the place. We are both very tired, and have another eleven hours to go till Visby. Gordon has looked after me well and it is once again my turn to take over from him. We just heard the Swedish weather forecast announcing an extensive low on its way to Scandinavia, a taste of things to come! The further north we get the more light there will be in the evenings, something that suits us just fine.

23rd May, 2000

It is past midnight and we are approaching Gotland, with Store Karlsö to starboard. The prospect of another landfall is making our adrenalin flow. We have to watch our course carefully as a strong current is offsetting us. Visby became one of the most important trading centres of Europe in the tenth and eleventh centuries, a time in which the island of Gotland changed hands many times, between the Swedes and the Danes and the Russians, most recently in 1808. From where we are, we can already see the thirteenth-century towers and walls. There is a permanent minefield around the entrance of Visby harbour. A boat like ours or any other vessel approaching in a thunderstorm does so at its own risk. Also, for the same reason, anchoring and fishing are strictly forbidden. The harbour entrance is narrow and should not be approached in a south-westerly gale.

At 7am, having been on the go for forty-eight hours, we finally secured our lines in Visby's harbour. Slowly we are getting more practice at night sailing and are less tired than we used to be. Now that we have arrived in the central Baltic we shall have to make sure not to listen to weather forecasts of the southern Baltic, a mistake easily made! We rested, after which we visited the medieval churches, ate shrimps and drank wine, all this whilst the weather worsened as predicted. After much homework and bending over charts Gordon decided that our landfall tomorrow would be Arkösund, some sixty-five miles from Visby.

24th May, 2000

At 8am we sail out of Visby and start to prepare *Fereale* for the force seven winds forecast. This is the first time that we have had a favourable wind direction, only possibly a bit more of it than we would have liked! We are slightly apprehensive but OK, and can already feel the change in the air. The Aries, our self-steering gear, is having to work hard for its living. Arkösund here we come. With the wind behind us the boat is rolling quite a bit but neither of us is feeling sick. Anyone not used to this needs a very strong stomach! A huge ship has just kindly diverted its course for us. *Fereale* is veering quite a bit but her speed is tremendous for her weight of fourteen tons. The owner of a Swedish boat in the harbour asked if our boat was new, a great compliment for this twenty-year-old girl. He came from Fårö, an island just north of Gotland, and was the first sailing vessel to arrive there this summer.

The waves are not as big as in the North Sea, but we are going like thunder. From the chart, the coast we are approaching looks scary and is scattered with rocks and islands. It is two weeks now since we left Den Helder; we have done alright to have come this far. The waves breaking astern of us are making a thunderous noise, and we are glad not to be heading into them. They are fast and shoot underneath and past us. We take turns to catnap in this vast open space, still without the hazards of the Swedish coast. The wind is still on the up and we have to watch our course carefully, as there is a large but insufficiently charted area marked on the coast just south and north of us. Now and again we surf on a wave until it brakes underneath our bow. *Fereale* is doing well but only as long as she is guided. I will be pleased when we are safely tucked away in harbour tonight. To get a good sensation of our speed you need to look through the portholes down below and watch the sea rush by. It is cold out there and after having been down below to warm up, I had to gather some courage before venturing out on deck again. Our energy levels shot up, however, after some hot chocolate and cheese on toast.

It is 4pm and we have been listening to the BBC's World Service and the weather forecasts on the local VHF coastal channels. Now and again it is important to have a sail like this, in order to raise our expertise, and gain confidence in *Fereale*'s ability. Now, though, it is best not to look astern. Time to go down below, take off my wet gear and change into a different set off waterproofs, more suitable for working on deck. The radar picked out our lighthouse before we did, and in bad visibility we just about managed to spot the marker buoys to guide us in. Tired, and after twelve hours of intense sailing, we arrived in Arkösund's small attractive harbour. Salty and damp, we shall attempt to sleep with the sound of screeching seagulls. At times we fret when in harbour, yet when in a bad sea we long for shelter.

25th May, 2000
It is early in the morning and the cockpit is filled with drying waterproofs. Down below the place looks untidy, with washing hanging everywhere. The wind is strong and cold, but taking the inland route will give us some flat water,

sheltered by the islands. We will probably only do forty out of the eighty or so nautical miles to Stockholm. Gordon is happy and singing to music in the saloon. I called Mum, who told me that she has bought a chart and is mapping out our course with each and every landfall, and our children are doing the same. Once on the way both of us are in awe of the beautiful scenery, a minefield of dangers in reality. The island to starboard is a nature reserve for birds and seals.

We sailed on longer than intended and arrived in Oxelösund by four in the afternoon, having had our daily dose of adrenalin, as usual, with the fog closing

in on us. Progress has been made, though, as we have now arrived in the northern part of the Baltic Sea. The sailing season here is from June through to September, but July and August are the best months when the sea has warmed up and there is almost constant daylight. We are pleased not to have got stuck in Visby, and to be in more sheltered surroundings now. On a darker note, our first sign of a problem appeared in the engine room; a possible leak in the exhaust, to be investigated further in the morning!

Typical overnight anchorage, Swedish style

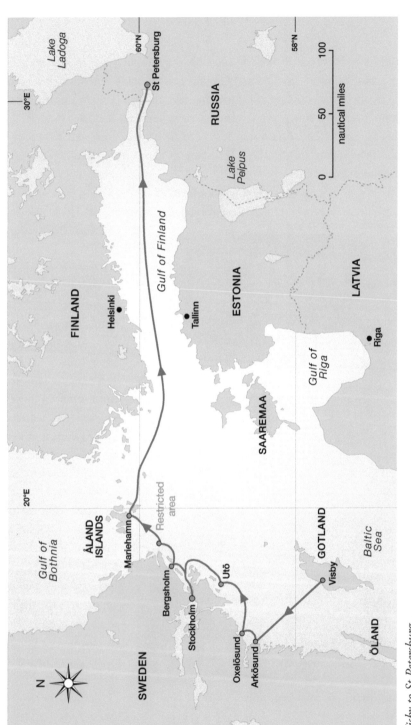

Visby to St Petersburg

Exhaust Problems

26th May, 2000

A full force eight is howling around us, and it is quite clear that we can't leave Oxelösund today. The barometer looks alarming, but the coffee is on and we are snug down below. It is nice having a little television. Even though we can't understand the language fully, we can still understand the local weather map. It looks as though we need to find a welder somewhere, as it has become clear that the exhaust pipe in the engine room has sprung a leak. Like this, life challenges us from time to time, throwing the odd obstacle in our way. Before long an appointment was made for the next day, allowing us time to move the boat in readiness. A day that started so nicely, when a local postman offered us a lift into town, finished with not only a broken exhaust, but also a faulty generator. Gordon is wracking his brains and looking through all the manuals he can find on the subject. Somehow he has to find a solution for our problems. I am keeping quiet in the background so as not to distract him. At 10pm the sudden sound of the generator's engine became music to our ears and all the pain endured became worthwhile. We often get asked by people what we do with ourselves on board all day, and the answer should be 'at times just surviving!'

27th May, 2000

The gale force winds having subsided, we motored the boat very gently to where the welder had his workshop. Every time the engine goes on black soot comes out of the broken exhaust, which blackens the engine room. The people here could not be friendlier, like the man who introduced us to the welder, for instance. He, himself, lived on his boat for nine years and sailed to East Africa, the Caribbean and the United States, earning his living on the way as a carpenter. Our welder, reluctant to weld inside our engine room, insisted quite rightly on doing the job in his workshop. A huge dismantling task lay ahead for Gordon, with locals going out of their way to help. Someone took him by car to a ramshackle workshop, where new gaskets were cut on the spot for no payment at all. We seem to be climbing up a mountain, as after the repair was made and all was back in place it leaked worse than before. By then our man had left for the weekend. I wonder what else lies in store for us, as we are unable to stay here for the weekend and need to make our way to Stockholm. We shall just have to use our engine as little as possible.

28th May, 2000
Carrying just a small Yankee and a reefed main, we set off at 8am. The wind is still strong and occasionally I have to go below to stow things better. A cupboard in the galley has just flown open, spilling its contents all over the floor. Harbours create a false sense of security! We are doing some eight knots, which is fast for *Fereale*. Having forgotten to put down the rudder of our Aries, we are forced to hand steer, with conditions too dangerous for hanging over the stern (lesson number one). Whilst I was hand steering and concentrating on our course, and Gordon bent over charts, I got the shock of my life. A huge ship passed close to starboard, one I hadn't seen, and far too close for our liking (lesson number two). After five hours of hand steering, Gordon finally braved the aft deck and sorted out the Aries rudder. With a gale on our tail, a lee shore and rocks everywhere, our chart suddenly disappeared underneath and behind our cockpit's sliding hatchway, a place we thought well suited to lay the chart, protected from wind and rain (lesson number three). For the first time in my life I watched Gordon turn panic-stricken and white in colour. Whatever we tried, we could not get hold of the chart and frantically Gordon started to dismantle the entire hatchway to the saloon. Tools were everywhere whilst I steered towards the one remaining waypoint. The courses Gordon plots into the GPS are always safe, and I was surprised to find a rock in my path. I told Gordon I was going to gybe the boat. He told me, in no uncertain terms, not to do so. But what else could I do? He had not seen what I had, and was too busy

to come and to look for himself. I went against his wishes and gybed *Fereale*. A shudder went down my spine as the sail came across and I felt the inside of my hands burning. Dismayed, Gordon came on deck to discover I had crossed into the path of a submarine. Like a flash of lightning we gybed the boat back, after which the submarine passed within only a few yards to port (lesson number four). We knew that there was a lot of naval activity, but the area was not restricted for the likes of us. After what seemed like ages, I suddenly saw the tip of the chart from the corner of my eye and we were saved just in time before reaching our last waypoint. The thought of heading back the way we had come in these conditions would have been unthinkable. Suddenly we knew where we were again, and our lesson learned was never to keep important charts on the lid of our hatchway. Our next job was to put the boat back together, put the tools away and sail to Utö. One of the many islands in the Stockholm archipelago, it is where one can still find the oldest and most important mines of Sweden.

29th May, 2000
After intense preparations we left Utö and sailed away. With the depression not over yet, we once again have gale force winds on our tail. As we thread ourselves in-between the beautiful islands towards Stockholm, protected from the heavy seas, we suddenly realise that by the time we have finished our round trip, we will have sailed the seven seas: The Zuiderzee, Waddenzee (Wadden Sea), Noordzee (North Sea), Oostzee (Baltic Sea), White Sea, Barents Sea and Norwegian Sea. We are on the approach to Stockholm now, a city on the water, with ferries passing us on their way to Mariehamn in the Åland Islands, Estonia, St Petersburg and Helsinki. With great difficulty we moored up to the pontoon in the still unrelenting gale, stern to a buoy. Our strength put to the test till the very end.

30th May, 2000
With a knock on the boat we were woken from our sleep. It was our harbour master informing us that we were in the wrong place; a spot reserved for the Royal Fleet. The Emperor of Japan and his wife were due to be taken out in one of the royal barges. They certainly had not picked a good day for this, and with aching muscles Gordon and I set about moving *Fereale*. Soon the royal barge arrived, covered in gold and manned by forty young oarsmen, an impressive

sight.

Although the harbour fees are expensive here, they include free washing machines, water and showers, of which I took full advantage and washed the entire cotton contents of the boat, including the upholstery.

After lunch we took a ferry to the old city of Stockholm where we went to an agent where charts and pilot books were waiting for collection. We cycled through the ancient town, filled with tourists and lined with craft shops. It feels very strange behaving like tourists, yet enjoying the comfort of our own home and transport. It is evening now and, although both of us are tired, we cracked open our last bottle of wine.

31st May, 2000

After the horrible job of putting covers back on cushions, we cycled through Stockholm, alive and buzzing with truckloads of graduating students, and paid a visit to the Vasa Museum. The Vasa warship went down in 1628 on her maiden voyage, owing to a design fault. The King of Sweden, who wanted to rule the Baltic, built her to help fight Poland and most of his neighbours. But her design was too high and narrow, something he was warned about and chose to ignore. Whilst still in the Stockholm archipelago the wind took hold, after which she heeled, filled and sank. It was not until some three hundred and thirty-three years later that she was raised from the bottom of the sea. I certainly hope *Fereale*'s Dutch design is better.

Time to look at charts and prepare for tomorrow's departure. The barometer has been steadily rising and finally the depression has passed. We are looking forward to being on the move again and are ready for our next adventure, and making another landfall. Stockholm will stay engraved in our minds as a charming town.

1st June, 2000

By 10am we were sailing through the skerries into Stockholm's archipelago, with the problem of our exhaust over for the time being. The smoke in our engine room proved to be caused by the newness of the weld. In another month's time we will have reached the White Sea and Belomorsk, with scenery very different from that of now. Today is a bank holiday, and everyone is out on the water. Having taken the inland route, we are enjoying the most idyllic sailing ever. Who wants to sail anywhere else on this planet? Jokingly we say to each other, 'what a hard life, not sure if we can take any more of this.'

It is nearly 7pm and finally we are moored up next to some other boats, with our bow to the rocks and the stern held by our anchor. At first we did not want to invade the privacy of the other boat and looked for a place elsewhere. Our unsuccessful attempts were observed by a couple of people from their private island. Seeing a Dutch flag and wanting to help, they jumped into their boat and told us to follow. This we did and ended up going to where the others were after all. We were told not to worry, as anywhere else wasn't safe. It is delightful here and the reason we enjoy sailing. I am confused as, when I try out my Norwegian, the Swedes tell me how good my Swedish is. There must be something wrong somewhere!

I had only just got into bed when we received visitors. Just in time I managed to rush back into my clothes and throw everything untidy underneath the bedding. The two men who had directed us to our spot had arrived in a little boat, carrying a bottle of rum. They were keen to meet these serious-looking sailors, they said. One of them was a Polish captain called Wojchiec, who teaches navigation in Stockholm. A man of many talents, whose hobbies are writing and painting. Then there was Törbjörn, a Swede, who owned the island nearby, and worked with something related to taps and brochures. Wojchiec moved to Sweden in 1980, banned from his own country by the communists. He told us how he'd had to buy back his wife and children, a struggle that took many years. They showed us nice places to go on the chart and seemed familiar with every rock in the area. Törbjörn, who spends every weekend on his island, winter and summer, told us how much he loved living here, and that no one in their lifetime could see all there is to see. In winter the ice is strong enough for him to drive to his island; in summer all he needs to do is call for a water taxi on his mobile. They left at midnight, after lots of gin, tonics and rum, and disappeared quietly into the sunset.

2nd June, 2000

Gordon has discovered a leak in the water-cooling system of our engine; a reason, perhaps, for the unexplained water in the bilges. We really should be on our way, and feel our peace has been shattered. Suddenly *Fereale*'s intestines are turned inside out, and like a doctor Gordon is trying to bring her back to life. At times like this he hates the boat, with tools everywhere and litres and litres of water in the bilges. His hands, which for days have had plasters on every fingertip, are once again in a dreadful state. We don't talk much, and quietly one bucket of water after another gets handed to me from the engine room. The birds, meanwhile, are singing and the swans begging for food. Our friends on the island must wonder why we have not yet left. It seemed such a simple job, but *Fereale* is complicated and everything inside her is difficult to get at. Last night Wojchiec described boats to me. "They are like women," he said, "all similar and yet so different. I love them." At 2pm the moment of truth had come and *Fereale* had been given the kiss of life. Not until five were we on our way to a nearby island, famous for its wild orchids.

3rd June, 2000
Time to find the orchids our friends had talked about, an opportunity not to be missed. Leaving Gordon to his chores I set off full of hope. Further and further afield I wandered into the densely wooded island, until I became hopelessly lost. It took ages before I found my bearings and was back on board, not having spotted one little orchid. We soon hoisted anchor and were off, but I noticed something was very wrong. Too scared to tell Gordon, after all he had been through, I asked him to take over from me. He discovered for himself that the rudder was jammed, and that we had no steerage way. Once again the controls were turned off, whilst Gordon dived down below. There he was to discover that in his haste to tidy up the engine room he had overlooked a cloth lying on the workbench. It had managed to get itself firmly wrapped around our steering cable. Whilst Gordon dealt with the problem all I could do was watch *Fereale* drift towards the busy inland route, counting our blessings that it wasn't towards the rocks. There was no way in these depths that we could drop anchor. Our problem was solved only just in time before we were in more open water where there was less traffic. On we moved and this time towards the last group of islands south of Söderarm Lighthouse. It was a place that Törbjörn said he had visited many times. It took hours to find a suitable island to safely moor up to, after which we discovered that we were in a military zone. How could Törbjörn suggest such a place, however beautiful? Nothing other than a rocket was going to move us, we thought. But the wind got up and unrelentingly pulled at our lines, our anchor failed to hold ground and soon

we touched the rocks below. It was not until 2am that *Fereale* was safe, and we were finally able to get some sleep.

Finland, Åland

4th June, 2000

There is a heavy swell and with every wave *Fereale* dips her bow into the waves. At 2pm we were able to hoist the Åland courtesy flag and sailed into the Finnish archipelago. Having had more practice now at picking up stern anchor buoys, things went smoothly. Even the formalities with custom officials were simple and easy. It is delightful here, and so peaceful, but in fourteen days' time it will be different as it will be mid-summer. The islands where we were last night could have been just anywhere, the North Pole for instance; it is so very different here. Just to make sure that we don't get too relaxed, our electric water pump stopped working. Still being able to pump water by hand, it was put on the 'to do' list.

Most of the foreign boats we see here are based in Finland, their owners flying out in summer. In the evening Gordon had a sauna, where he nursed his arm and shoulder, both suffering from tendonitis. Basically he needs a long rest, away from all the hard labour-intensive tasks. The sun is setting behind the pine trees and complete stillness is surrounding us.

5th June, 2000

It is cold inside, and a strong northerly wind is blowing straight into our cockpit. Gordon, having inspected the water pump, finished fitting a new one by 6pm. It is time to move to the diesel pontoon and fill up. Our intention is to leave tomorrow, both of us wishing we could stay longer. As always, staying in harbours for too long tends to get expensive. Whilst dealing with the ropes and fenders, I was unaware that Gordon was experiencing problems with the reverse gear. He wondered if he was paranoid, but when coming into the diesel berth her gears failed completely. I jumped ashore, and managed just in time to stop the boat bumping into a wall. *Fereale* surviving with only a little scratch to her paintwork! How lucky we had been, but Mariehamn was not a place for mechanics, as we soon found out. Our gearbox, having been serviced in Holland before we left, was as good as new. Is this new worry with the gears going to stop us meeting our deadline in St Petersburg, or will we end up sailing the Baltic instead?

6th June, 2000

During the night Gordon's shoulder and arm were causing him a lot of pain and I watched him struggle to get comfortable. His hands, and particularly his fingers, were swollen and cracked. With bandages soaked in soda, I wrapped each of his fingers, covering them with the cut off tops from sterile gloves. A treatment that worked, but one that had to be endured day and night to stop infection. Gordon, having called our dealer, Kemper van Twist, in Holland, was given three possibilities of where to look. With that he set to work and discovered that possibility number two was our problem; a couple of broken gear levers, the broken bits of which had fallen into the gearbox. Next a fax was prepared on our computer giving Kemper van Twist instructions to send the parts by courier. My mother, our lifeline as always, was going to make sure that they were paid. Both harbour master and son could not have been more helpful and understanding either. So much for cruising around Finland as it looks more and more likely we will be sailing straight to St Petersburg from here. *Fereale* is telling us to hold on and that all hope is not lost. Gordon, fishing for the broken bits with a magnet from my sewing box has found one little part of the puzzle. He needs a different tool, one that can bend, as he is worried about losing the magnet in the gearbox. It is important to find all the bits and not to clog up the hydraulic oil pump. In the meantime the harbour is filled with small children running around, or sailing their Optimist dinghies. We are more relaxed now, and have resigned ourselves to the fact that we can do no more and will accept whatever happens.

7th June, 2000
Another day has passed, and it is pouring with rain. Our harbour master, who keeps us well informed, has told us that the weather is going to change for the worse. Our plan, if at all possible, is to leave at the weekend, and we hope that it won't be the weather that will be stopping us this time. We can't stay here for very long if we are to meet our deadline in St Petersburg. A local mechanic, whose second job is being a coastguard, took Gordon to a shop where he was able to buy just the right tool. With raised hopes, he started fishing for the broken bits and completed the jigsaw within the hour. With the knowledge that the spare levers were on their way by courier, and having been told that they would arrive the next day, things were looking up. Outside it is blowing a gale, but fortunately we have a short memory concerning bad weather, and try to remember only the good days. Life on board is simple and very physical; the finest cure for overwrought nerves. To make good use of our time the engine was switched on to heat the oil, in readiness for an oil change. But whilst sipping tea in the cockpit, a horrible thought came to Gordon's mind. Suddenly he got up, switched off the engine, and dived down below. He was confronted with an absolute nightmare. With a half-smile on his face, he could not believe how stupid he had been. Having only just topped up the gearbox with red hydraulic oil, he had not yet put the lid on and the entire engine room was covered in what looked like blood.

Thick fog has descended over Mariehamn. It is time to look at the charts once more and plan our route to St Petersburg, the city of white nights and the marine capital of Russia. There are millions of islands in Finland a long way out to sea, and it is important to get well clear of them if either of us is to get some rest. Fog is our biggest worry. In the evening, Gordon braved the sauna, together with the locals. It is a social event here in Finland, and where, presumably, stories of the sea are exchanged.

8th June, 2000
I am not very well, and have threatening bronchitis. By the weekend, though, I should be feeling a lot better. The *Pommern*, moored up right next to us, is one of the last big sailing vessels before the steamers took over, needing fewer crew members. So far we have not done any sightseeing, but this was an opportunity neither of us wanted to miss. In 1939 the *Pommern* was laid up in Mariehamn,

having sailed for the very last time. Her task in life had been to ship cargo between Europe and South America. In 1953 she was donated to Mariehamn, and ever since local craftsmen have kept her in shape. Once a year, when the weather is calm, her brand-new set of handmade sails gets hoisted, and she is able to show herself off. Down below everything is still in its original state, and we were shown films of the *Pommern* sailing in horrendous storms. The matching soundtracks made me feel uneasy, with the North Cape in my mind. Quickly I managed to pull Gordon away and moved on.

Whilst strolling back to our boat Gordon pointed to a beautiful sailing yacht entering our harbour. It was gleaming all over with bright varnish work and carried a white ensign! The members of crew wore the same clothing and looked very smart. "Only the Royal Navy and the Royal Yacht Squadron have the right to fly that ensign," Gordon said. A privilege vigorously protected with substantial fines for offenders. It is a facet of English culture that people get very snobbish about the ensign they fly from the stern of their boat. Unlike us, of course, who are flying the Dutch colours! Later in the day, having seen that the white ensign had been replaced with a red one, Gordon questioned our harbour master. He asked what had happened and if he had been aware of the meaning of the flag. "I have just about seen everything," he said, "but not this one." He went on to explain that it had been the coastguard who had made them take it down, that they had been warned that Mariehamn was a military-sensitive area in which foreign naval vessels were not permitted. This news cheered Gordon up no end, and he considered it worth our week's delay to have witnessed it.

We ended up having a nice chat with our harbour master and were told that he lived not very far away, on one of Åland's six-and-a-half thousand named islands. He told us that there were many more that had not been named. He just loves living here, like every local you meet. What a blessing. "Come back," he said, "you are always welcome." How we wished we could do just that.

9th June, 2000
As we had hoped the spare parts arrived by 9am, at which point Gordon dived into work. In the meantime I scrubbed the boat and topped up with water, water that was to last us all the way through Russia. Just as he had finished, Mum called. Pleased with the good news, she asked if we intended to leave

Transfusion for the gearbox

the same day. We would have liked to do just that, but Gordon had literally worked his swollen and open fingers to the bone. One more night I told her, not wanting to give the real reason why. In the sauna he took the time to nurse his aching limbs, after which he soaked his hands in soda, a sorry sight once bandaged up. Force six was due from the south tomorrow, and once out at sea *Fereale* should charge along. From incoming emails we learned about problems some of the other boats in the fleet were experiencing; we were not the only ones having a hard time. We heard of a blown cylinder gasket, a torn jib,

Gordon's next boat

bad weather, and near encounters with submarines. Let's hope that the boats waiting for repairs in Stockholm would make it to St Petersburg in time.

It is cold, and the wind is blowing straight into the cockpit. I feel restless and am unable to sleep.

10th June, 2000

It is Saturday morning and after clearing customs we left Mariehamn. We are committed to sailing all the way to St Petersburg and can't make another stop, unless we are willing to go through the whole procedure again. It is a good thing we have a second GPS, as the one in our cockpit is having difficulty finding the satellites, a problem Gordon is not sure how to fix. We are beating into the waves trying to get away from the islands. *Fereale* does not like this very much, and neither do we. If we had the courage to go in between the islands we could have avoided all of this, but that would have been one complication too many. Not until we point into the right direction towards St Petersburg will we get a more comfortable ride. It is sickening down below, something we shall have to endure for another two hours at least.

Before we left we were able to inform the remainder of the fleet via email of our whereabouts. Still in Tallinn, Estonia, they had worried about us, having heard about the storms in our area. They had emailed us, they said, but had not received replies. My Psion palmtop computer unfortunately stops working from time to time, but for the moment everyone is happy. Inge and Richard have also been in touch and we are looking forward to meeting them in St Petersburg. They, as always, have a lot of faith in us, the fools, but we really would not have it any other way. If they didn't have faith, we would not and should not be doing this trip.

In another hour we will be clear of the rocks, and should be able to sail a better course. It is definitely more comfortable now that we are in deeper water. Gordon has gone down to his bunk and will, I hope, be able to sleep for the next three hours. The Aries has taken over from the hand steering, leaving me to plot the hourly positions, write up the log and keep a good eye on our course. There are gale warnings ahead, not a pleasant outlook. Securely clipped and not carrying much sail my watch proved not to be an easy one. This was due to our faulty cockpit GPS, making me go down below to check our ground course on the other instrument. In Mariehamn we tanked up with good water for the last time, and we shall have to be very careful with our supply. All dishes, for that reason will have to wait till tomorrow. Every ten minutes the coastguard calls up various ships in the vicinity, and I listen to their conversations on suggested channels. The ships are asked for their call sign, port of departure and destination. All so very friendly, after which they wish each other a good watch and a safe voyage. I would not mind a little chat myself.

11th June, 2000
Neither of us slept very well on our first night out at sea. This is usually the case, but today will be better and tonight better still. The wind has died down and the sun is high in the sky. I have just woken Gordon, tempting him with coffee in the pot. We look after each other well, something so important. He trusts me with his life, he says, something I knew but love to hear! Tallinn radio just warned of gales in the Gulf of Finland and other areas. The only good thing is that the direction of the wind will be south or south-west. At least we should be flying! We need to prepare well, and get as much rest as possible.

For a while now we thought we could hear thunder, but realised what it actually was when we saw gunboats. The chart shows that we are sailing along the edge of a naval practice area. Six fearful-looking warships are practising their firing skills at targets in the water. For some time we have watched a sailing boat going the same way as ourselves, and realise she could be in danger. She is right in the middle of it all, with shells exploding all around her. The navy called them up on Channel 16, and this is how we found out she was a British yacht called *Kate*. They were told in no uncertain terms to get out of the danger area. *Kate* is also bound for St Petersburg like us, but is not going any further into Russia. Gordon, having called them up on the VHF, found out that they carried old charts, charts that did not show the latest naval practice area. Offering some assistance with waypoints, they chatted for a while. I felt quite envious that they were stopping off at Helsinki, as unlike us they were in no hurry to get to St Petersburg.

With lots of time spent looking over charts it hasn't been a good day really. Both of us feel unsettled and are unable to sleep, even when conditions allow us to. It is just like Piccadilly Circus, with many ships converging here from the major ports of Tallinn in Estonia, Helsinki in Finland and St Petersburg in Russia. We shall have to be very careful. Before the Berlin Wall came down in

1989-1990, it was impossible to visit Estonia, still ruled by Russia. But after the collapse of the Soviet Empire, countries like Estonia, Latvia and Lithuania became independent. All of these countries are looking to better themselves and want to join the EEC, and trade with Scandinavia.

I have now been on watch for two hours and hope to go on till midnight. There is a change in the weather, and the boat is covered with thunder flies, fog has descended and navigating is intense.

Entering Russia

12th June, 2000
It is 5am and we are preparing *Fereale* for the gale force winds about to confront us. Yesterday's forecast did not materialise, but no doubt it will today. I managed to get four hours of sleep, which Gordon tells me has been put into my piggy bank to spend as I wish. He is hoping, of course, to get the same amount of sleep himself. Suddenly there is thunder in the air and our radar shows the rainsqualls rushing towards us from astern. Quickly, I covered our radar display and VHF and disconnected the antennae, but the squall came and went like the many others that followed. I was woken up with the news from Gordon that the Russian courtesy flag had been hoisted, and was told to have a look at the forbidding-looking island of Ostrov Gogland. An island with no friendly little houses, but military buildings and radio towers instead. The bad weather we are having makes it look more menacing than it really is. Carefully we watch the current, as there are dramatic changes in the mountainous landscape of the sea below. Both of us are scanning the horizon for a cardinal buoy that is supposed to be there but isn't, a phenomenon we will come across more often. The hatches are firmly tied down in case one of the following monster waves crashes into our cockpit. I had quite forgotten how frightening they look. However much I prepare myself when gybing the boat, the force of the mainsheet coming across always surprises me. Shocked after a sharp shudder down my spine, I am recovering with my hands still burning inside the fishermen's gloves.

Not wanting to arrive in Kronstadt harbour in the middle of the night, we tried sailing under bare poles to slow *Fereale* down. Perhaps there will be rusty old jetties to tie up to, something not to be contemplated in the dark. But, for the Aries to cope, however, *Fereale* needs a more balanced rig, so we hoisted our bright orange storm jib for the very first time. All of this could be quite scary, but both of us were calm and ready for a long and difficult night.

The only port of entry into Russia is the island town of Kronstadt in St Petersburg harbour, where we have to stop for customs clearance. Yachtsmen following the rules precisely should not have any problems. I am trying not to look astern, and realise that even should I try to take a picture it would not portray the reality. We don't have a wind indicator and can only guess that it must have reached a full force nine by now. Real character forming stuff, this! One can't sail these seas without believing in God, and all we can do is ask Him not to give us more than we can handle. To sail to the north you need a certain passion, different to a hobby. It is lovely to arrive with your own floating home in an area where other people don't usually venture. The seas here don't see many sailing vessels, as roughly only twenty foreign yachts a year reach St Petersburg.

13th June, 2000

It is time to call the Russian coastguard on the VHF and make them aware of our intended arrival. Both of us are up, as it is not a good idea to be alone in the cockpit at this time. Gordon has to laugh as, even in the roughest of conditions, my diary is by my side. On the edge of a huge shipping lane, we follow the narrow channels, unable to see over the top of the waves ahead. The wind is howling more than ever, but *Fereale* is nicely canvassed, and balanced. I am tired and unable to sleep owing to the motion of the boat, and my bronchitis. Gordon is most frustrated by the fact that I don't look after myself well enough in these conditions and has firmly positioned me in the shelter of the hatchway and told me to stay there. It is 2am and to keep our spirits up Irish music is filling our cockpit; a dramatic sea shanty of *Ships on the Rocks*. Perhaps we were not quite meant to hear this particular song, but both of us have to laugh. The big ships that pass us must think we are mad, all of them are rushing to catch the opening times of the St Petersburg's night bridges; bridges we will also have to go under when our time comes.

The last bit was truly horrendous, and with boiling seas we entered the harbour of Kronstadt, situated at the mouth of the Neva River. Having steered by hand for the last few miles, we had been unaware that our wind vane had broken in half. Safely, we managed to lower the sails in reasonably protected waters, and tie up alongside the customs office. Curiously I watched a young Russian official who helped take our lines. Not even a hint of a smile was to be seen on his face; no smile of welcome. But we are meeting different cultures after all, and this is what it is all about. Part of our adventure is discovering. A heavily made-up lady in uniform, with gold-capped teeth, boarded *Fereale*. With gestures and unspoken words, she took our passports, visas and crew list. Then there was a lot of coming and going of officials, one of them obviously drunk. All went smoothly as the Cruising Association's Honorary Local Representative, Vladimir Ivankiv, whom we had emailed, had given the authorities warning of our estimated time of arrival.

Just as we had arranged to stay for one night and I was about to take a nap, Brenda and Alan arrived in their Victoria 38 called *Nomad*. This was our second time meeting them, the first being at the convention in Reading in preparation for our trip. They had waited for us in Helsinki, they said, where it had been agreed that we would meet up. Our plans, however, had changed dramatically since Mariehamn. It was wonderful to see them, and we will sail many more miles together. Not being as tired as us, they were keen to continue on to St Petersburg. Not a bad sounding idea, and only another two or three more hours after all.

The route to St Petersburg is not a canal, but a buoyed channel through the Nevskaya Guba waters. Not very deep, and therefore rough, with short waves, a bit like the IJsselmeer in Holland. The approach to a city on the water is always amazing. St Petersburg turned Petrograd, turned Leningrad, turned St Petersburg once more, is located in the delta of the Neva River on the shore of the Gulf of Finland. Hydrofoils, like stick insects, go to and fro, not even touching the water. We managed to safely tie up at the Central River Yacht Club, to a pontoon full of gaps and made out of dubious-looking planks. The clubhouse was a modern unfinished building, with deterioration overtaking the slow rate of construction. I felt as if we had climbed Mount Everest but, little did we know, we had only just reached the foothills. Whilst having a celebratory drink on board *Nomad*, Vladimir Ivankiv and the press arrived. Not having had a chance to wash my hair, or feel in anyway refreshed, I was horrified at the thought of being interviewed. All we wanted to do was sleep, and so did Brenda and Alan. Fully understanding, Vladimir kindly asked them to leave and come back some other time. He had not known, of course, that we had sailed all the way from the Åland Islands in Finland without stopping.

On watch, Gulf of Finland, en route to St Petersburg

Central River Yacht Club, St Petersburg

VESSEL REPORT / CREW LIST

NAME OF VESSEL: TYPE:

REGISTRATION NUMBER: WEIGHT:

NATIONALITY OF VESSEL: HOME PORT:

PORT OF DEPARTURE: ....   DATE..../..../....   TIME: ....

DESTINATION: ....   DATE..../..../....   TIME: ....

PORT OF RETURN: ....   DATE..../..../....   TIME: ....

CAPTAIN'S NAME:

DATE OF BIRTH: NATIONALITY:

PASSPORT NUMBER:

ADDRESS:

NAME OF CREW:

DATE OF BIRTH: NATIONALITY:

PASSPORT NUMBER:

NAME OF CREW:

DATE OF BIRTH: NATIONALITY:

PASSPORT NUMBER:

CAPTAIN'S SIGNATURE: ....

FOR OFFICIAL USE:

St Petersburg

14th June, 2000

In the morning we were shown Vladimir Ivankiv's office in the Central River Yacht Club. From the outside the building looked impressive, but inside the clubhouse was bare, with big holes in the plasterwork. It was built in 1980, when St Petersburg was in competition with Tallinn for hosting the Olympic Games. Tallinn won, however, and since then there has been no money available for the building's maintenance. Vladimir, who is an account manager for the club, has had to borrow money in anticipation of earned revenue from the visiting fleet. He has made a huge effort to accommodate the likes of us with toilet and shower facilities, all basic but adequate. The weather is still unrelenting and I am concerned for the rest of the fleet. Gordon, however, does not share my feelings, and tells me that if they have made it to this side of the Baltic, they are perfectly capable of looking after themselves. He is right of course.

It did not take long before we saw four more boats coming in, and not only were we pleased to see them, but they were delighted to see us too. The skippers and crew enjoyed a wonderful lunch in the clubhouse, consisting of soup, bread and beer, all for the grand price of $1 per head. It was there that we heard the terrible news that Nick from *Brough Sands* had died of a heart attack whilst still in Holland. We were shocked, and so was the entire fleet. Once back on board I lit a candle for him; he and his wife had worked so hard, like all of us, to make a dream come true.

With our daughter, Inge, and her husband, Richard, arriving tomorrow at noon, I shall have to put my thinking cap on, tidy up the boat and create some much needed space. I had only just finished when there was a knock on the boat. Some Russians were keen to come on board. It was Michou, a Russian sailor, Vladimir Yermakova and Vladimir Gromov. It took me a little while to make the connection, but all of them were organisers of the festival, together with Vladimir Ivankiv. They were kind and offered help with any problems we might have. It has been through their efforts, and that of the Cruising Association, that sailing through Russia has been made possible at all.

15th June, 2000

Gordon and Vladimir Ivankiv are trying to find out where to buy two hundred litres of purified bottled water. Our leftover supply has suddenly become like gold dust, and I have labelled the taps in the galley as such. From now on the water on board can only be used for drinking and cooking; clothes are to be washed on the quayside with rusty tap water. Whilst waiting for Inge and Richard, we also need to find out where to refill one of our gas bottles. Together with the chart preparations, there is plenty to do.

After a delayed train ride and a taxi driver unable to find our harbour, Inge and Richard finally arrived. We hugged and were so pleased to see them. They had come all this way to share our Russian experience from St Petersburg to Petrozavodsk. Leaving them no time to unpack, we hopped onto a trolley bus with some borrowed roubles. One of the skippers asked if we could change some English pounds for him, when in town. A huge amount in fact, and something we lived to regret dearly. The wallet Gordon carried was attached to his belt and able to hold what cash we needed, but little had we thought of where to put the extra roubles. Already in the bank, we felt probing eyes upon us, and the shopping that needed doing was done quick and fast. "Let's get back to the boat," Gordon said with all that extra cash. The journey took longer than expected, a nice sightseeing tour taking an hour and a half. Like fools we had jumped on the right bus, only to find out a lot later that we were going the opposite way. Back on board Gordon made the discovery that he had been robbed of all the extra cash in his pocket. Our friend, no doubt pleased that he had not gone into town himself, was handed over the equivalent, but money that was ours instead. Speaking to someone else about it, I got the answer: "Life is like roulette, you win some, you lose some; it will come back to you in another way." He is right of course, but it did not make me feel much better. An invitation from Inge and Richard to eat at the club that night at their expense soon made us feel better. Back on board at last, where we were handed the many letters from relatives and friends waiting for us to read. Unable to do so, and overwhelmed by the happenings of the last few days, I went to bed exhausted.

16th June, 2000
We have been told that there will be an inspection of all the boats going through St Petersburg. The pilots quite rightly want to see if the boats they are to board have strong enough engines. Engines that can push against the strong counter current we are to expect in the river. We waited and waited, wasting a lot of precious time, only to find out that after they had checked three boats they had seen enough. There is great tension amongst the skippers of the fleet, some heavily disputing the money the pilots will be charging us. For a while now I have been looking for Gordon, who disappeared some time ago in search of diesel. By the time Inge and Richard came back from town he was still not back and in my imagination I saw him hurt or in the water. Richard, perhaps thinking I was over reacting, nevertheless joined me in my search and together we walked along the riverside calling out from time to time. On our return we noticed Gordon walking back towards *Fereale* in clothes that were not his. I was right, it seemed he had fallen in the water whilst trying to help Ray on *Babaji*. A lifeline on a Russian boat had given way, one that he had assumed was strong but wasn't. A whisky soon made him feel better and helped him to forget about his badly bruised arm and open sores. Next we all pulled together and filled our water tanks with the forty or so containers of purified water that had arrived.

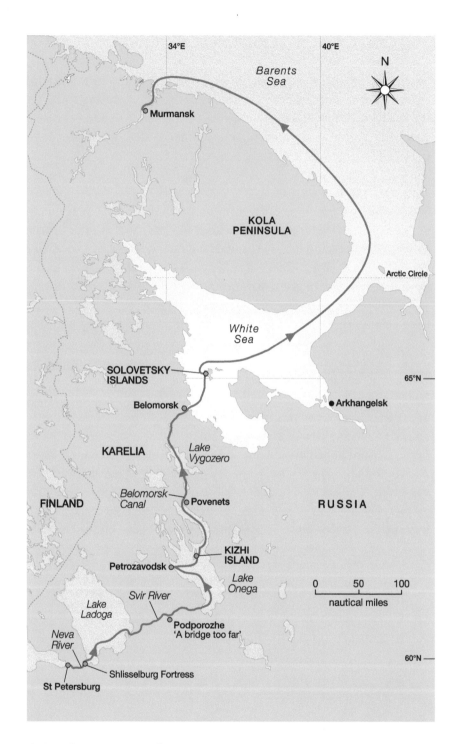

St Petersburg to Murmansk

Striptease

17th June, 2000

In the pouring rain Inge and Richard, together with all skippers and crew, left for a sightseeing tour of St Petersburg. We would have liked to join them, but Gordon still had an oil change to do, and I had to think of how to feed five people for the next five days—we had heard that Vladimir Gromov was to join *Fereale* all the way to Petrozavodsk. Changing the oil was not as easy as Gordon had hoped. With a badly wrenched arm from yesterday's fall, and ripped skin on the palms of his hands, I watched his desperate attempts. The filter, situated in a most inaccessible place, would not budge, once again an ultimate test of endurance and nerves. But, by using his engineering mind, the job was eventually done. Time for a good night out, and this is exactly what we had.

In a nearby beer tent we met the rest of the fleet and joined them for some food at long wooden benches and tables. Gordon laughingly pointed out to me that there were bras hanging from the wall. I myself had noticed during the course of the evening how a long barrelled rifle had been carried into the tent and hung on the wall behind the bar. It was not till after dinner that we discovered that we had entered a striptease tent. Much to the delight of the vodka-fuelled sailors, a beautiful young Russian girl did her act and stripped down to nothing. The sailors could not believe their luck and any barriers that might have existed were gone, language and otherwise.

All of us had been invited to attend a balalaika performance in the clubhouse after dinner, but few attended. Unable to draw our men away, Inge and I dutifully trotted off to the clubhouse where we had a wonderful time. From a distance we could hear our men's laughter coming from the tent. Inge, slightly embarrassed by this and tired from all the travelling, decided to retire to *Fereale*, leaving me to get our men back somehow. Not an easy task! With my arms around them both they just about managed to avoid the many gaps in the pontoon on our way back to the boat. How they got on board and managed to walk the tightrope to *Fereale*'s bow I will never know. Gordon and Richard had not only had a couple of drinks but had survived a Russian drinking competition, which is no mean feat. Our first night out in Russia!

A local takes a shine to Gordon

Richard, second from the left, enjoying himself with the locals in the famous tent

18th June, 2000

The ten boats, by now having been given their schedules, were told to assemble by the first bridge in the 'Small Neva' at 11pm. This is where we would be introduced to our pilot, for him to join *Fereale* properly just before the opening of the first bridge at 2am.

A very strong current runs through the bridges of St Petersburg. Approximately fifty cargo ships of up to five thousand tons will be going through at the same time as our fleet. I have been making use of my time by cooking tonight's evening meal, as there will be six of us on board including the pilot.

One of the boats has already left and is waiting by the bridge. We have been told to follow a boat called *Onega*; she is the one that will be guiding us around the shallows. Vladimir Gromov kindly brought with him some chicken and sausages, a very welcome treat. It is now midnight, and there is still some daylight left. The boats are waiting patiently for the ten pilots to board. Going through the eight bridges of St Petersburg will take us about two hours, beyond that the Neva River is seventy-six kilometres long. We have now left and our pilots have boarded. They are concerned about one of the boats in the fleet, which is going too slowly for their liking. A small Russian tug is staying close by to help should any of us get into trouble. By now the current is very strong, and our pilot is telling Gordon when to turn to port or starboard. Sign language is sufficient, but of course we have Vladimir Gromov with us who is able to translate. There is a full moon and we have just passed Lenin's palace, a very memorable occasion. As we push ourselves upriver one bridge after another is opening for the large cargo ships and our little convoy. It is one of the most special moments of my life. Even the pilot and Vladimir are moved, by the fact that our countries have joined together.

We have now passed four bridges and are tied up alongside a large ship at anchor. Its sailors asked if they could come on board and have their picture taken. Of course they could, and I watched their proud faces as they stood by *Fereale*'s mast. Vladimir is very happy, as all is going very well so far. He, together with many others, put in a lot of effort so that everything would run as smoothly as possible.

On our way again and the pilot is looking tense with concentration. With his own radio by his side he is continuously in contact with the other pilots, large ships and bridge keepers. It is an immense responsibility for him to guide us through safely, as they are not used to little boats like us. Their job is to guide huge five-thousand-ton ships through St Petersburg on a nightly basis; ships whose engines are strong, ships that hardly notice the current. The current against us is five knots, and the pilot is telling Gordon to increase his speed in order to maintain steerageway. Suddenly it looks as if there are problems. Our pilot heard over his radio that *Babaji's* engine had stopped. It is amazing as all the boats in the fleet flocked around her, and I feel touched by this gesture. In fact the engine had just overheated, and Ray needed to slow down. A tense moment for us all. If anything goes wrong for anyone, we are all in the soup.

19th June, 2000

It is 10am and Inge and I have been on watch for the last couple of hours. We have just dropped anchor and are waiting for the opening of a bridge. It seems that a huge passenger cruise ship has to go through first. All of us had only just dropped our anchors when we were told to lift them again in a hurry and go through the bridge after all. Unexpected things like this happen all the time and there is not much time to relax. Excitedly I waved the Dutch flag at the four men operating the moving parts of the bridge. Seeing ten foreign sailing boats must be a unique sight for them, one that happens only every ten years, perhaps. Vladimir has woken up and is having a wash by the sink in the galley. I wonder how I can possibly wash myself in private, with every space on board occupied.

The banks of the Neva River don't look very interesting, and the factories and cranes along the shore are all old and decrepit. There are five boats in the fleet with shorter masts than us. They do not have to wait for the bridges to open and have gone ahead. At 3pm we dropped our anchor near Shlisselburg Fortress but Vladimir, intent on giving all of us a good time, was not happy with the arrangement. Determined to get us all ashore to see the sights, he managed to get an invitation from the local mayor for the boats to come alongside the quay in the village. Up went our anchors once more, which was no problem for the boats with electric anchor winches, of course. Many official-looking people paraded the shore showing off their authority. The mayor had obviously organised security. It did not take long before the skippers and crew were ferried on a local boat to Shlisselburg Fortress, situated on an island nearby. For four hundred years the castle, dating back to the sixteenth century, and with impressive six-metre-thick walls, had been a prison. In the seventeenth century the Swedes conquered the island, which they then owned for ninety years, but in the eighteenth century Russia finally won it back after a heavy battle fought by Peter the Great. We were shown the prison cells, still in their original state, and it was easy to imagine the horrendous conditions of that time. Gordon, who had not joined our expedition, had to stay behind in order to give *Fereale*'s engine some attention. Too exhausted to cook that night, our crew had to be content with soup and toast, after which we collapsed into our bunks. Which is where, in spite of our nets, the mosquitoes feasted on our blood.

Lake Ladoga

20th June, 2000

It is very nice to see that when the fleet is told by the pilot to depart by a certain time everyone is ready. By 7am we were on our way to Lake Ladoga. Mind you, getting up was hard and Inge and Richard did well to stay in bed. Having five people walking around, wanting to wash and have breakfast all at the same time is too much. Both of them are fully aware that they will have a more peaceful time if they get up later.

We are now on Lake Ladoga, Europe's largest lake, which covers an area of eighteen thousand square kilometres. The distance we have to cover is 110 km. Not far away there are a couple of elk trying to reach the shore. After a desperate attempt they finally managed to get a foothold and disappeared into the reeds. More than thirty rivers supply Lake Ladoga, yet only one river, the Neva, flows from it. The lake is St Petersburg's main source of drinking water. The weather is uneventful and calm, but in the winter the conditions can be quite different here, with swells of up to six metres high. Vladimir is trying to sleep in the saloon this time, having not found our passage berth very comfortable. Tomorrow it is Inge's birthday and, whilst Richard and I were on watch, I quickly dug out her present and some decorations. We will be sailing through the night and it will be the strangest birthday she has ever had, but a special one we hope!

Gordon is not very happy. Our one remaining pilot, the one on board *Nefertiti*, seems to be cutting corners and passing cardinal buoys on the wrong side. When questioned he tells us not to worry and says that there is enough water to do so. Whether right or wrong we are not used to navigating in this way, and Gordon has decided not to follow. From now on he is sticking to his own course and intuition. Sometimes it is as if we are on a flotilla holiday. The agreed Channel 77 is getting used for the most mundane announcements or questions put to Vladimir by the rally fleet, giving us not a minute's peace. In desperation we switch to Channel 16 only. *Spirit of Aeolus*, most concerned about our silence, made a huge detour to check if we were OK.

We are now in the Svir River, a river that connects Europe's largest lakes; Ladoga, to the west, and Onega to the east. Richard has been steering for the last couple of hours and it is midnight. The scenery is breathtaking! The next bridge is not opening until eight in the morning and in order not to have to hang around for too long we are slowing down. *Minos*, the boat we are in convoy with, has decided to do the same. The balloons and decorations are up, and we are ready to celebrate Inge's 29th birthday when she wakes.

21st June, 2000
We are now in Karelia. The early morning mist is hanging above the water, and the sunrise is producing wonderful colours in the sky. On either side of

Inge & Richard, Lake Ladoga

us are little islands, and woods filled with pine and fir trees. The main source of income for the people living along the Svir is lumber. On the odd occasion when there is a sign of life, we see piles of logs and storage sheds along the shore. We need to keep a good lookout, as there are lots of tree trunks floating in the water. Vladimir, unable to sleep, has wrapped himself up in a blanket and is lying on the aft deck. Whilst I was dead to the world a birthday song came over on the VHF for Inge, from the rest of the fleet. I rushed to my feet and noticed that many of the boats had dressed overall for the occasion, and on *Spirit of Aeolus* the code flags showed: 'Happy Birthday Inge 29'. Elsbeth had even made a birthday cake.

Nearly 2pm and finally the bridge has opened for us. "There were mechanical problems," Vladimir said. He continued on to say that the bridges were only opening because all of us had paid and that our fleet was paving the way for others to follow. We are all very happy to be on the move once more, especially Vladimir, the co-ordinator of the festival. It is his mission to see to it that all of us reach Petrozavodsk safely, and in time for the opening of the Blue Onega – 2000 festival, a yearly event since Russia first opened its internal waterways for non-commercial vessels in 1994.

On we go to Lake Onega, with no more stops until we reach Petrozavodsk some sixty nautical miles away. We have been told that Lake Onega consists of natural spring water and that we can top up our water tanks there. We are all curious, as it is difficult to imagine filling our tanks from buckets dunked over the side! Parts of the lake never freeze in winter, as the pressure from the natural springs at the bottom of the lake keep the water turbulent. Whilst waiting for the lock to open Gordon mentioned that he had noticed something strange with our gear lever, that it somehow felt different. But with the birthday festivities in full swing, the problem was put aside. When we finally lifted our anchor, however, I noticed that the engine was not engaging. Gordon quickly took over, after which the gear engaged, but only for a minute or so. Not until we were in the lock itself did it become apparent that our cable had broken. As quick as a flash Vladimir jumped ashore and managed to rig a towline from *Spirit of Aeolus* ahead of us, as the lock gates were already opening. Next we were towed out; the birthday celebrations having come to an abrupt end.

With Richard at the helm, Gordon and Vladimir took the steering column apart. I myself was saying silent prayers whilst preparing our dinner with Inge's

Village life along the river

help. The repair only took half an hour, after which the men could relax once more and enjoy the scenery. To my amazement, Gordon had managed to repair the cable by turning it end for end. For once the noise of the engine was music to our ears. Vladimir, misunderstanding Elsbeth's hand signals telling us to slow down, cast off the towing line instead. For a minute there was panic on board *Spirit*, as the twenty-five metres of rope trailing from their stern threatened to foul their propeller. At full speed they circled round and round until they finally retrieved their line. Inge and Richard have discovered by now what life on board of *Fereale* can be like; how our strength is continuously tested and super human efforts are required at times. Arriving at our anchorage we heard clapping from the rest of the fleet. They were so pleased to see that we had survived this one, as none of the boats carried spare cables. I bet that from now on they will all carry spares, just like us.

22nd June, 2000
We had been told that it was early to rise if we were to catch the opening of the railway bridge at 7am, but seven came and went and became five in the afternoon. *Fereale* in the meantime had moved closer to the bridge and had rafted up next to *Minos*. Our peace was short lived, however, as the hydraulic gates had been

opened causing a strong current. The two boats rafted up together dragged their anchors and both touched the bottom. If they were to reduce the flow of the water at the floodgates for us it would mean that Moscow would have less electricity. People would then complain and go to the top. Whilst waiting patiently we were informed that no permission had been granted for the bridge to open. Vladimir was terribly worried and spent most of his time on board *Spirit* discussing the situation with our pilot. He desperately had to make a phone call to Petrozavodsk to keep them informed of our delay. A delay for Vladimir meant that his job could be on the line, as the festival's success was based on the arrival of our fleet. A delay for the boats meant that our food supplies were running low, and that some of the boats' crew might not make their pre-booked return flights home. But Vladimir managed to solve that problem also,

and in various dinghies they went ashore. Always wanting to help, Vladimir, Inge, Richard and other members of crew went ashore in dinghies to hunt for food. It did not take long before Vladimir had managed to persuade a shopkeeper's wife to open up her container of stores. There they found eggs, bread, onions, tomatoes and vodka and, most importantly for Vladimir, a slice of pork fat. Far away from the big cities the people are doing just fine and nobody goes hungry. Here one doesn't plan a menu and buy the ingredients; rather one finds the ingredients and

The first of the slow bridges

then plans the menu. On his return Vladimir made the comment that his countrymen had not recognised him as a Russian, owing to his western clothes. They had treated him differently until they found out that he was one of them. He told me how much he would like to live here, as the people were kind and helpful. "Something rare in Russia," he said, and not always the case where he comes from.

Vladimir managed to make a call to Petrozavodsk, but it was hard for him as he himself could not be contacted owing to the absence of a telephone network for our mobiles. He told me that if he did not manage to get us to Petrozavodsk in time the officials there would never want to work with him again.

The bridges here never have to open for anyone, as all the big cargo ships manage to pass underneath. They are not used to sailing boats with tall masts. This particular bridge had not been opened in years and in having to do so they came across huge mechanical problems. *Minos*, who had stayed near the bridge at anchor, informed us by VHF that the army was present and that he had heard the sound of hammering.

Suddenly Vladimir arrived in a little dinghy with an outboard alongside *Fereale*. Together with David from *Nefertiti*, they had arrived to collect Gordon. Vladimir announced that he was hoping to save the bridge. He wanted to call their bluff and take an engineer along with forty years' experience. Gordon, feeling slightly flattered by this, quickly got together pen, paper, tape and torch, to do the pretend bit! At the last minute I managed to hand him our hand-held VHF, just in case, together with our binoculars. Off they went, speeding up the Svir River against a strong current and towards the bridge. It was not long before we heard Gordon's voice over the VHF. "Rally fleet, rally fleet this is *Rubber Duck*." In David's excitement *Rubber Duck* had hit a rock and the men were marooned ashore with a broken engine. *Minos* was the first boat to react and quickly pulled up anchor. The idea was that *Rubber Duck* would paddle to the middle of the river coinciding with a pick-up from *Minos* at the right moment.

From then on all went well, even though we had lost radio contact. The men, relieved that *Minos* was going to take them back, had walked to a workshop at the foot of the embankment. There they found two soldiers from the Frontier Regiment, one of them flat on his back clutching an empty bottle of vodka. Vladimir, who had hoped to do some negotiating, was livid, and his patience had clearly run out. He slapped the man's face in the hope to bring him to his senses, a gesture that was obviously not appreciated. Angry at being woken up in this manner, he asked Vladimir to identify himself, which he duly did. But this did not seem to satisfy our soldier, who turned to his superior and asked permission to shoot the three men. Of course all of this was in Russian and Gordon and David could only guess what was happening at the time. "Go ahead," Vladimir said, "and shoot me if you like." Luckily the lieutenant had more substance between his ears. He told Vladimir where he could find a telephone and what was required to get things moving. Together they climbed the embankment and Vladimir set off down the railway track in search of a telephone, from which he rattled the cages of the bureaucrats. He is the fleet's lifeline, as not only does he deal with the river authorities, but the pilots and railway companies as well.

Vladimir was soon to leave our company. Even though we stay together as a fleet, psychologically it means a lot for him to be on a faster boat. Also, he needs to be seen on the first boat, to arrive in Petrozavodsk, and not to be at the back of the fleet, *Fereale*'s preferred position. On *Spirit of Aeolus*, he will be more comfortable also, and will be able to shower, have his own cabin and put his dirty washing in the machine.

By midnight he had managed to rock the system and told us that he had taken the matter right to the top. He had called associates of Yeltsin, he said, as this was the only way to get the bridge to open for foreign-flagged vessels. Whilst Moscow was asleep, and therefore needed less electricity, it would be possible to allow less water through the floodgates. At last the moment had come and we were told to weigh anchor, but as we turned the key in the ignition nothing happened. Richard was straight away instructed to lower it once more whilst I got onto the VHF. Looking around me I had seen that the fleet was already well on their way to the bridge. Explaining our problem to Vladimir, he calmly replied that he had just been informed of another delay, of approximately forty minutes. Gordon sprang into action, with Inge by his side. Richard and I in the meantime handled communications on deck with *Spirit* and *Nefertiti*, who were hovering nearby. Both of them had offered us a tow if needed, and a line was prepared just in case. It was obvious that our starter battery had failed. Our generator, with its own battery supply, worked fine. Bags, mattresses and bedding flew through the air. It was the only way for Gordon to get to the main batteries underneath the passage bunk. After the longest twenty minutes ever, the sound of the engine was not only music to our ears, but the entire fleet. Gordon had jump-started the engine with leads to the domestic batteries. We should have had Simon and Garfunkel's tape on board, *Bridge Over Troubled Water*.

Excitedly I waved the Dutch flag and blew the foghorn as we went underneath the bridge. I had heard that most of the people from the village had helped to get it up. For us it was a special moment, but not for all of the boats in the fleet. Some were annoyed, that it had taken as long as it did. It will be a much longer time, though, before the enormous bureaucratic hassles are ironed out. I don't think there will ever be a moment when one can expect to sail through Russia without an agent or a pilot. Let's hope that the boats that follow in the future can take more time to enjoy what they are seeing, and will be allowed to sail the lakes. We ourselves feel rushed and have barely had time to breathe. All of us have to be in Petrozavodsk by a certain time. I have also been told that Vladimir's boss and our pilots are not keen for them to be away for too long. I take my hat off to Vladimir, who has to accommodate everyone in the fleet—the most difficult task of all. I have heard him say that he will never do it again, but know that it was said in the heat of the moment.

The last time this particular bridge opened was six years ago, back in 1994, when the Dutch Coastal Cruising Association organised a sailing rally to Russia. The voyage was dedicated to the 300th anniversary of the Russian Fleet and 400th anniversary of the start of Willem Barentsz' expedition to the north of Russia. Their trip was in the reverse order to ours, as they went first via the Norwegian west coast and then around the most northern point in Europe, the North Cape. Once they had reached the Russian border some local English-speaking sailors joined them, and together they sailed across the White Sea to Archangel. From there they followed the newly opened inland waterways to St Petersburg, and finally went westward, across the Baltic seas, to Holland. Thirteen boats in all participated in that rally.

I think that anybody who wants to sail through Russia on their own, or as part of a fleet, will need to be prepared to take on board Russian crew for the entire trip. If your boat is small, for instance, this might be a problem, but it is one that can't be avoided. Your Russian crew will be able to help you out of many an awkward situation.

64

Petrozavodsk / Karelia

23rd June, 2000

Today we should arrive in Petrozavodsk if all goes to plan. Lots of crew changes will take place. We will sadly lose Inge and Richard but will gain Colin, Gordon's brother, as a crew. He is arriving by train from St Petersburg in the early morning. In convoy we are moving full speed ahead. Inge and I are keeping watch and hope to give our men a well-deserved rest. Miles and miles of forest can be seen along the shore, with trees that look like soldiers standing proudly in the water. I have heard that bears, foxes and elk prowl these forests and I scan the shore eagerly in the hope of seeing something. Once in a blue moon we see a small village along the shore, its houses built of logs. It is a cold and lonely place. By the time Inge and I woke up we were entering Lake Onega, which covers an area of some ten thousand square kilometres. In winter the lake is frozen for at least six months. Not until we reach Kizhi Island will we find the best of the fresh water springs. There we hope to top up our depleted tanks with the purest water, from a lake not yet polluted by humankind. It's time to do the washing and thoroughly scrub the decks, as tomorrow at 10am we will be hosting Russian guests and want to look our very best. It is wonderful to have Inge and Richard as eager deckhands, to do all the hard work for us. The crystal-clear water tastes sweet and soft. Slowly we skirt along the west coast of the lake, to arrive in Petrozavodsk, the capital of Karelia, at just after midnight. One third of our voyage now complete.

Washday on Lake Onega

24th June, 2000

Moored bows to the shore and with stern anchors, the boats lay side-by-side in a small, unkept dock area. To celebrate our arrival all the boats had dressed overall, which was a lovely sight. Alarmed, we watched *Babaji* entering the harbour and about to hit the rocks, having misunderstood the buoyage. Only just in time she heard our call on the VHF and understood our frantic hand signals. Vladimir Gromov, thrilled that his flock had arrived in time, soon arranged security for the boats. Vladimir Yermakova was also there. He had travelled by train from St Petersburg. A special edition newspaper had informed the entire city of Petrozavodsk of the fleet's arrival. In order for the thousands of people to get a good view of the boats we all had to move to a different spot. This time we were tied up alongside an attractive waterfront park, nicely landscaped with lawns and flowerbeds, benches and walkways. The Russian strollers that came by all gawked across the railings at our expensive-looking western yachts with their strange, foreign flags. Before long the ten boats were motoring in line along the shores of Petrozavodsk. It was a bit like a beauty contest, with *Spirit of Aeolus* in front, followed by *Nefertiti*, *Reflections*, *Nomad*, *Law Dance*, *Minos*, *Endring*, *Fereale*, *Nuada* and *Babaji*. As each boat

Midnight arrival at Petrozavodsk

passed a certain point along the shore the mayor of the town announced to the public who we were and where we came from over a loudspeaker. Owing to our starter battery problem we had declined having guests on board, just in case, but nevertheless Vladimir's wife and son became *Fereale*'s guests of honour. *Nefertiti* and *Spirit of Aeolus*, the biggest boats in our fleet, each entertained many important officials. Loud music came from the speakers on the banks of the shore and, once back, television crews and photographers milled around. The arranged security was good, and three soldiers stood guard over the boats. It is exactly two hundred and ninety-four years ago today that Peter the Great founded the shipyards here. It is also commemoration day for the people that died during the Second World War.

Someone dressed up as Peter the Great arrived with his followers to welcome us, and parachutists fell from the sky carrying huge banners. It was spectacular. The locals that strolled by were well dressed, in current western fashions, and with attractive hairstyles. The young girls were adorned with big bows and had ribbons in their hair, and looked healthy and well fed. We had been lucky that our engine had started, but knew that we would not be able to continue without a new starter battery. Michou, who had also travelled from St Petersburg, soon

The arrival of Peter the Great

offered to help us. With the compliments of the festival organisers a car and driver were arranged, and Gordon and Michou were taken to one of the few places open that day. Gordon worked like mad whilst everyone else enjoyed themselves, praying that the fault was with the battery and not elsewhere. At last all was well, but both of us had missed all the activities of the day. Not so for Inge and Richard, though, who together with the others were taken on an excursion around Petrozavodsk, to a concert and much else.

Ready to have a good time, Gordon and I managed to join the beer festival in the evening, together with the others in the clubhouse. On the way, Vladimir showed us an open boat without an engine, in which he and many oarsmen had sailed all the way from Russia to Spain about ten years ago. Finally we arrived at a hulk of a barge (the clubhouse), totally hidden amongst the many strange-looking wooden shacks. We were amazed to find it so beautiful inside. Wooden tables lined the walls and a model ship decorated the centre of the room. Peter the Great and some Vikings arrived to entertain us, showing us how they did battle in the ninth century. All of us had to applaud in rhythm. In the ninth, tenth and eleventh centuries such warriors defeated many enemies and invaded many countries. "Cheers to Europe," they chanted, "Petrozavodsk and Karelia!"

Disaster

Colin was collected from the train station by the two Vladimirs, who drove him to the dock area, where he joined *Fereale* in the early morning. With Inge and Richard still on board, he was assigned the passage berth. It was lovely to see him, and once we had introduced him to the rest of the fleet it was back to business. We were told that we could obtain diesel and possibly water nearby. None of the boats wanted water, as we were all looking forward to filling our tanks from the lake. When it was our turn to tank up, we were told to moor up behind the diesel barge where we were handed a big black hose. After some two hundred litres, we realised that it was the water hose we had been handed and not the diesel. We just could not believe it; this was the biggest disaster that could have happened and it felt as if a bomb had hit us. But it did not take long before Gordon was in survival mode and a barge had been found willing to take our fouled diesel for $20 in return. With the transfer pump, a long hose and Colin's help the diesel was transferred directly into a container on the Russian vessel. Soon the word had spread, as more of the rally boats after us had needed diesel. It hurt me deep inside that nobody apart from Vladimir had offered assistance, whether this was needed or not. All were keen not to miss their second day of entertainment by the Russians. No doubt they thought us pretty stupid, and quite rightly so. I had insisted that Inge and Richard, on their last day in Petrozavodsk, would represent us and join in with the others on the guided tour through the city. There was not a lot they could do for us after all. Taking a little stroll to clear my head, and absorb what had happened, I found

71

a wooden log. Thinking I was alone, I sat down and let my tears flow freely.

To my dismay I found out that I had been watched, and on my way back to the boat I was kidnapped! Just before stepping on board *Fereale* a kind-looking Russian, a little younger than myself, approached me. Not speaking any English, he made gestures that I was to follow him, and offered me his hand. By now every Russian in the dock had heard about what had happened. Feeling that he was just going to show me something a few yards away I went with him, not wanting to be rude. He firmly held on to my hand, and together we climbed from one ship onto another and eventually his. I was wondering what was happening, but never felt threatened or unsafe, not until I was led into the galley of his huge freighter, where two men were watching a pornographic film. Seeing that I was clearly embarrassed by this, they kindly turned it off. Next I was told to sit down, after which I was offered a full glass of vodka, which I gratefully declined. To do so, however, was rude, and they were having none of it. Suggesting perhaps a smaller glass, I was offered still a huge amount by my standards. I think he felt sorry for me and wanted to cheer me up, having seen that I was sad. Just taking a little sip was not accepted either and I was shown how to knock it back. Not wanting to be rude, I did as I was told. They desperately wanted to talk to me and find out where we had come from. So many questions, none of which I was able to answer. Next I was given toast with what looked like raw fish. I knew very well that these gestures came from the kindness of their hearts and ate what I was offered, shuddering inside at the taste. They were kind but I had made clear that I needed to return to the boat, knowing full well that neither Gordon nor Colin would have noticed my absence. Delighted at being understood, my friend took me by the hand once more but, instead of turning right—the way we had come, he turned left and we ended up in the engine room. There was an engine the size of *Fereale*. I was impressed. It made me feel small, and I watched him start the engine by hand especially for me. Pistons went up and down and from it came a lovely sound. Everything was so well nurtured and cared for. He was proud of his ship, which was so many times the size of *Fereale*. I had the feeling that he was the only engineer on board and our problems suddenly seemed small. It proved to be the right medicine, after which I was safely guided back to *Fereale* and felt ready to face the world.

Gordon hadn't missed me one little bit. In fact, he had thought that I had been asleep in one of the cabins! When our main tank had been emptied as much as Gordon was able, we moved on to the diesel barge to tank up. On taking a sample from the bottom of our day tank, Gordon found out to his dismay that water was still present. The barge that had taken our water-infested diesel, however, had moved away. Straight away we cast off our lines and managed to find them just around the corner of the harbour on an outside berth, where we repeated the process. I asked Gordon for some help in explaining the function of a day tank, as not every boat has one. Only too pleased to give his input, he told me that all diesel engines take their fuel from storage tanks. In most yachts these are located low down in the bilges in order to help stability. A pump is then used to lift the fuel to the engine above. If the fuel is stored in more than one tank in the bilges, valves are required to switch from one diesel supply to the other. These valves unfortunately interrupt the flow to the engine. Also, if the tanks are particularly low down it can sometimes be difficult to prime the pump. With a header tank (day tank) this problem does not occur, as the engine will get its fuel by gravity, rather than the fuel having to be lifted by the fuel pump. This is the set up on *Fereale*, with the added advantage of a sump that collects most of the sediment or water that may accumulate in the fuel.

Exhausted from all the hard work in the intense heat, we moved *Fereale* back to her berth where Inge and Richard soon joined us after their trip into town. The iron came out and in a hurry we prepared ourselves for our night out to an official dinner we hadn't expected to be able to attend. It was Inge and Richard's last night with us, and Colin's first. The spread of food was wonderful and was laid out over long tables in the most grandiose style. Our men looked so smart in their blue blazers and ties, and the ladies didn't look too bad either. In fact, none of us could be recognised from our former selves. But during the dinner and speeches the piece of toast with fish that I had eaten on the freighter turned sour in my stomach and I had an urgent need to get back to the boat. A mini bus, assigned to the skippers and crew, brought Inge, myself and a few others back to the dock. The men, having been told to attend yet another meeting after dinner, made their own way back.

Stepping aboard I noticed a stranger on one of the boats next to us and called out to him. He was carrying a plastic bag half filled with possible goodies, which alarmed me. Seeing him leave in a hurry I decided to give chase and in my long skirt tried to get around the fence he had disappeared behind.

Watching my struggles, a concerned Inge took over the chase. It did not take long before she returned having lost him. I was furious. Where was the security all of us had been promised? Had anything been stolen from the boats? I had noticed a smartly-dressed man who, without helping, had observed all that had happened. Perhaps a bit rudely I walked up to him and asked him who he was, to which he replied that he was a friend of Vladimir and that he was waiting for him. Delighted at the fact that he spoke English, I asked him to join me in my search for the security man. We eventually found our man in a nearby hut, sitting in front of a television and very drunk. "Has anything been stolen?" asked my translator. "I don't know," I replied. It was a hopeless case until everyone had returned and checked their boats. Once back on board we waited for the skippers. The best reward for me was that none of the boats had been broken into and that I had obviously caught him at the start of his intended burglary. The bag must have contained things from elsewhere. At last I was able to rest and nurse my upset stomach!

26th June, 2000
It is 6am and Gordon, already in his overalls, is draining water from the bottom of the day tank. This is best done when the boat is not moving otherwise any water left in the diesel will mix with the rest. When stationary it sinks to the bottom of the tank and Gordon can drain it off. Bags are everywhere, as Inge and Richard are packing in readiness to take a hydrofoil to Kizhi Island, where we will part company. Colin, having slept his first night in the passage berth, has been promoted to the aft cabin. By 9am the fleet was on the move, cutting their way across Lake Onega for the next thirty nautical miles.

Kizhi, only a day's sail away, is situated in the north-eastern region of Lake Onega. Sadly we are not allowed to sail, as together with the other boats we have to stick to a rigid schedule. *Nefertiti*, who has a pilot on board, is our leader. Vladimir is following us all on a tugboat together with the press. Horrendous, blood-drawing flies with huge teeth are attacking us in the cockpit, and a fight is on to protect ourselves from the nasty beasts. It is hot and hazy, and occasionally we see flashes of light. Nobody wants any food, as we don't want to take our eyes off the beautiful scenery surrounding us. From *Fereale*'s cockpit we can see the famous thirty-seven-metre-high Transfiguration Cathedral, with its twenty-two cupolas, built in 1714. As we get closer we were

Ladies of the lake

told over the VHF to anchor in the waters directly opposite. It is the first time ever that permission has been granted for foreign vessels to anchor there. From the island we can see Inge and Richard waving at us, having arrived a little while ago. One of the skippers, eager to row ashore, got a surprise when the oars of his dinghy were confiscated by the security people on the island. Apparently nobody is allowed to row ashore. Before long Vladimir had collected everybody from their boats, to be taken on a pre-arranged tour of the island, an island measuring six by one kilometres. Once we had met up with Inge and Richard we visited houses and barns built of logs and walked through fields of rye. Local girls in costume showed us how they made traditional necklaces and embroidered beautiful cloths. Later the girls gathered in a little boat and rowed away between the reeds singing enchanting Russian songs. It was a magical moment for us all, and one of the many highlights. The large houses we saw usually house about four families each. During the dark and cold winter months they eat and sleep together in one room, the only way to keep warm. In the few months of summer, however, the whole house gets used and they have all the space they need.

Churches of Transfiguration and Intercession

Unfortunately the circular interior of the Transfiguration Cathedral has been closed to visitors for the last few years owing to preservation works. But we were able to visit the Church of Intercession nearby, which housed the many beautiful icons from its closed neighbour. The architect of the cathedral was a carpenter called Nester, apparently. Legend has it that he threw his axe into the lake after completing his work, saying: "There never was such a church before, nor will there be any in the future," and he was right. Next there was the windmill, which, together with other interesting objects from different parts of the Republic, was brought

The cupolas are all tiled in timber

to Kizhi to show visitors how the peasants, hunters and craftsmen used to live. Its thirty-metre bell tower was built in 1874 and has a tent-shaped roof. A small cupola with an elegant cross on top crowns its structure.

The churches were full of wonderful icons

Windmill, Karelian style

So the time came for us to say goodbye to Inge and Richard. Better, though, in Kizhi than in Petrozavodsk. Here at least we were able to spend some time together, however short. Still with so much uncertainty ahead of us, and Inge and Richard more aware of what we had taken on, we hugged and kissed and said our goodbyes. Just as well neither of us had too much time to dwell as they, too, had to focus on what was ahead.

By now permission had been granted to row our dinghies to the shore, but first we had to move our boats to another anchorage. It seemed that the boats were not allowed to stay anywhere near the island for the night. Vladimir, on his special boat with the press, took us all back, after which we weighed anchor and followed him some fifteen nautical miles downriver. When safely anchored, we were once more collected, but this time by little open boats with fast outboard engines, which took us a few miles further downriver where we had tea at a local guesthouse. There the owner and his wife met us and all of us were given the grand tour. Our host kissed the hand of every lady, clearly delighted to be allowed to entertain us. The house and everything inside was homebuilt. He was a proud man and I quietly envied their life, quite un-influenced by our material world. There might be hardships, but I am sure that none of

them would exchange their lives for ours. In a room upstairs, overlooking the lake, we were given Russian honey cakes and dried fish, to be swallowed down with the most delicious tea, coming from the biggest teapot ever seen. Anna Yermakova, a Russian girl who had travelled with Vladimir to Kizhi, was our translator for the evening and, at only seventeen, she did her parents proud. But the horrendous flies were still bothering us, especially Gordon, whose blood they liked the most. In spite of being tempted with the offer of a sauna, we had to leave. We thanked our hosts and were quickly whisked back to

Anna

Fereale. Hurriedly we put up the nets and lit our mosquito coils, after which we slept well; unlike André and his crew who were tied up to a rotten wooden quay that night and were just about eaten alive.

27th June, 2000

Just when we thought we would be able to have a little lie-in we were given five minutes' notice on the VHF to raise our anchors. Colin, having let down all of our fifty metres of chain by mistake the night before, struggled to get our anchor up. Off we went, back to Kizhi, this time for an official breakfast. All of us had paid a lot of money in advance for this occasion. It was an opportunity for the fleet to say thank you to our Russian hosts for all they had done for us. To our surprise we were allowed to come into the harbour and moored up, bows to, with a stern anchor out. After bread, vodka, lots of speeches and goodwill we were given T-shirts and mugs. Vladimir had been invited to continue his journey on board *Spirit of Aeolus*, but accommodation still had to be found for Anna. We were told that the fleet needed two translators, Anna and Vladimir, and that each would need a salary of $10 per day. Being the only boat with possible room, we agreed to take her on board. All of this came as a

Fereale moored up for the official breakfast, Kizhi

A quiet evening near Kizhi

total surprise to Anna who, armed with no more than the clothes she stood up in, joined *Fereale*. I had met her once before in Petrozavodsk, with her dad, Vladimir Yermakova, one of the organisers of the festival. We were delighted to have her, as she took the place of our daughter who had just left. Colin was pleased not to have to give up his bunk in the aft cabin, as Anna—a lot smaller than him—fitted in the passage berth much better. Soon Anna and I, desperate to cool off, disappeared to find a place where we could swim on the island. We found a secluded and private spot where we swam in the clearest spring water ever seen. I had read that anyone who bathes on the island is ensured marriage within a year. Colin and Gordon, on seeing us so refreshed, joined us later for yet another swim.

It was time to say goodbye to the five boats returning to St Petersburg. The boats left to continue sailing through Russia and around the North Cape were *Fereale*, *Endring*, *Nomad*, *Spirit of Aeolus* and *Babaji*.

Endring is a ten-metre Gambling belonging to André Aas. André is Norwegian and a marine biologist by profession. He first heard about the possibility of sailing through Russia when he stumbled across Ray Glaister's homepage on the subject. He told me that sailing around something has always appealed to him. Sailing through Russia certainly seemed the easiest way to circumnavigate Norway. Ray Glaister's offer for him to join the fleet made the practicalities of it all a lot easier.

Nomad is a brand new but well-tested Victoria 38. She is sailed by Brenda and Alan Donaldson, a husband and wife team from Guernsey. "We are going to do that, and go the whole way," said Brenda to Alan when they first heard about the rally. Neither of them would have ever contemplated undertaking a voyage of such complexity and length without the back-up of the Cruising Association. Alan, having retired early, had explored the Baltic twice before, and many more places like the Orkneys, for instance. Together they make a great team.

Next comes *Spirit of Aeolus*, a beautiful boat owned by Willem and Elsbeth Vankerk. *Spirit* is sixteen metres long and has been built from aluminium. Both Willem and Elsbeth are Dutch but emigrated to Canada a long time ago. *Spirit* is Willem's dream boat, and one he designed himself, together with a naval architect from Massachusetts. She flies the British Virgin Islands flag and is a pilothouse cutter, with an aft cockpit. Having only just arrived in Holland

Refilling the water tanks in Lake Onega, using bed linen as a filter

after crossing the Atlantic, some friends of ours who happened to meet them made a mention of our plans. Without hesitation, they got in touch wanting to know more about it. It is wonderful how instantly one becomes friends when a dream can be shared.

Finally *Babaji*, a nine-and-a-half-metre motorsailer ketch, owned by Ray and Margo Glaister. A comfortable boat with a deck saloon, which allows the crew to stay inside, protected from the elements. *Babaji* and skipper are no strangers to Russia, as both have previously ventured as far as Moscow. The trip to sail through the inland waterways was really Ray's brainchild. Being aware of how difficult it is to get around North Cape and back in one season, Ray will be doing the logical thing. Having left *Babaji* in Finland last winter, his intention is to leave her in Narvik, Northern Norway, once he has rounded North Cape. This way the cruise will be nicely spread out for them over two seasons. Since we live on board and need to find work this is not an option for *Fereale*.

28th June, 2000
We were off at 7am, Gordon having checked the diesel for water first. Both of us feel pressurised by the pace of the agenda set by the Cruising Association

"Where are we?"
Chart conference approaching Povenets

but, to get around the North Cape and back in one season, a tight schedule is required if one does not want to get stuck in the ice or encounter bad weather. No bread had been available in Kizhi, or any other kind of food for that matter, so breakfast consisted of porridge, not something we would usually serve on a hot summer's day. At last we were able to fill our depleted water tanks. Draping a white sheet over a large bucket, Gordon and Colin started filtering the pure spring water from the lake, pulled up in buckets and siphoned into our tanks. This supply would have to last us all the way to Norway. Anna and I had a wonderful time, washing anything we could lay our hands on. She would at least able to sleep in clean sheets unlike before. Our spin dryer worked overtime, and it did not take long before everything was dry. Down in our saloon, Anna is relaxing. She loves drawing and made a sketch of the five boats, sailing amongst the islands. She also wrote a Russian poem for us, about a cat in a tree, and cooked pancakes for lunch.

With *Babaji* some distance behind and the others in front, we approached Povenets. Gordon and Colin, who were too busy chatting, had passed west of an east cardinal buoy by mistake. We had noticed that a couple of fishermen in a little open boat were shouting at us and waving their arms. Whereas Gordon thought they were just waving, Anna had understood what they were saying. "They are trying to warn us about the rocks," she said, after which Gordon realised his mistake. The engine was quickly put into neutral and slowly *Fereale* altered course. The only way to convince Anna that we were safe was to show her the charts, after which she stopped worrying. We were very grateful though, as she proved to be our guardian angel. When we finally rafted up next to *Nomad*, Brenda, who is a keen swimmer, was already in the water cleaning their boat. I could hardly wait to join her, but it did not take long before she had to give up, as one of her fingers had jumped out of its socket. "Oh, this happens from time to time," she said with a smile on her face whilst popping it back in its socket! It must have been so painful, but she was not going to show it. Always eager to help, Anna and Vladimir went in search of food for us, and came back with bread, chicken, eggs, chocolates and special biscuits, to top-up our meagre supply.

Stalin Canal

29th June, 2000

Every day seems to bring a new adventure and we are preparing for departure at 8am. Colin and Anna are swimming for the last time, since from now on the colour of the water will change dramatically, we think. Vladimir is collecting the pilot, who will guide us through the eight double locks of the infamous Belomorsk Canal. The canal, constructed during Stalin's rule in 1931, is two hundred and twenty-seven kilometres long and was built out of human bones, a past Russia does not like to talk about. It is Karelia's horror story as, for every metre of canal, one man died. At the end of a winter's working day, men with sledges would collect the bodies that were left behind. The bones that remained there till summer were ground together with the cement. The people that survived are still living today and are spread out over the whole of the Soviet Union. Not long ago, in the village of Povenets, near the Ladder of Locks, one hundred and thirty graves were found, holding more than nine thousand bodies.

Our pilot has given each boat a chart to cover the area, which we will have to hand back later. Alan and Gordon are searching the shore for suitable fender boards before we hit the locks. By 9am we left in convoy, with *Spirit* as mother duck and *Fereale* at the back of the fleet. We were told that it was at the first lock that the Russians had managed to stop the German progress into the Soviet Union. When we reached the second lock a kind lady handed us a bunch of wild flowers, after which I rushed down below to find some English tea to give her in return. Apparently we have to climb eighty-nine metres, and

The famous five await entry to the Stalin canal

then descend the same amount. We are all getting the hang of how to handle our boats in the locks and slowly, inch-by-inch, *Fereale* and the others climb the Povenets ladder. In the summer season, when the waters are not frozen, this route connects the Gulf of Finland with the Black Sea and the White Sea. It is going to take three or four days to pass through the canal, as there are some long distances in between. The boat ahead of us is very unpredictable and not easy to follow, one minute she slows right down, and the next she suddenly steams ahead. I can't say that we are particularly enjoying this, as it is all very tiring and not much fun. Not our idea of a holiday, but I suppose we knew that in advance. It is pioneering what we are doing, paving the way for others to follow. Anna, our figurehead, is sitting high up on the bow, her favourite place to be.

Our pilot has just told us that we are moving too slowly. It is the boat ahead of us, however, that is slowing us down. Not wanting to be rude in mentioning this over the VHF, we silently hoped that they would get the message. We anchored in the stretch of water just before the descending locks, where Anna swam to *Spirit of Aeolus*, as she wanted to be with Vladimir, her substitute dad, and the pilot. With them, she would be able to speak her mother tongue. We had to watch her carefully as the current was strong and it was quite a distance. So, for a while, it was just the three of us again, as Anna, quite rightly, decided not to swim back. On our way once more, with the pilot, on *Spirit*, guiding us in and around the dense population of beautiful islands. Colin and I are taking turns to steer *Fereale*, whilst Gordon is taking a nap on the foredeck. Being so close to the shore, the menacing flies are once more out to get us, however much we cover up.

We have reached lock number eight, and from now on will be going down the plughole—an eighty-nine-metre drop—over the next seven or eight double locks. Colin, who is quietly sitting in a corner, is catching up with his diary. He tells me that owing to the fact that there is so much happening, he has problems remembering the details. It seems unbelievable that it was only a few days ago we filled our diesel tank with water, and that we are making any progress at all. It is 6pm and there are still many locks ahead of us. It is hot and all of us are tired.

Just when I was trying to sleep on the foredeck, *Fereale* slowed down dramatically. Vladimir, at a time when the boats were doing six knots, had jumped unexpectedly from *Spirit*'s stern for his daily swim. Willem, quick as a flash, threw him a line with a fender attached and circled round at great speed, scared of fouling his propeller. But Vladimir, who was holding on for dear life, had greater concerns as his trunks by now were around his ankles. It was a comical sight for us onlookers. Vladimir, who has a bad back, needs his daily exercise. On board *Fereale* he used to do press-ups every day on our aft deck, but he never surprised us in this way.

At lock number four we stopped for the night, and Anna re-joined our ship. Delighted to see each other again, we both jumped in, where our bodies sizzled like hot pans in cold water.

30th June, 2000
We are confused. One minute the fleet was told by our pilot to hoist sail and do their own thing, only for him to change his mind the next. Too late, *Endring*, the Norwegian boat, had left already and was out of sight, having forgotten to switch on their VHF. Our pilot, very concerned about this, made us leave in a hurry, so we could catch up. André had had a wonderful time and was

Fending off   *Anna as a trainee line handler*

quite oblivious to it all when we finally caught up. He had had a few moments nobody could take away from him.

Anna and Gordon are in their respective bunks taking a nap. Colin and I are enjoying a coffee whilst navigating. In the afternoon we watched as *Spirit's* crew catch a huge fish, weighing some three kilos, and a second one not long after. Their shouts of delight could be heard far across the water. Encouraged by this, I had a go with my trailing line, but failed miserably! It was not until we reached Norway that I mastered the art. All in all we have gone through four double locks today and have dropped some thirty metres in height. These locks, unlike the others, are badly maintained. Quite pleased not to be the first ones in, we came alongside *Spirit*, who was tied to a dangerous-looking pontoon. The wind increased and the flies left, another hectic day has passed. André and Gordon are discussing where to go once we reach the White Sea, a place where our every move will be monitored by the military. I have quietly slipped away to our cabin, to sleep away what is left of the night.

1st July, 2000
Up early as always, as it is time for domestic chores and to think of what to eat today. Time to delve into my stock of food, spread out under various bunks.

Some local children offered Anna a wild mushroom

Will I catch a fish today? I wonder, but don't hold out much hope. Every morning Gordon's first job is to siphon out the water that has sunk to the bottom of the day tank, and check the filters. It is getting colder now and the steam is rising from the water as it cools off. It's a beautiful sight, but I hope the fog it creates won't close in too much. At 10am we left and had reached the beginning of the last four double locks by noon. The pilot always warns us in advance where to put our fenders; to port or starboard. This is a great help, and stops a last minute panic. Anna, wrapped up in a blanket on the saloon bunk has not talked since breakfast time. Perhaps she is having an off day. Colin, who is a great help, has taken over what is usually my job. I am not complaining. Only one side of the locks usually has bollards, which float up and down with the rise and fall of the water. It is hard to believe that the stretch of canal we are in at the moment has been dug manually. All of us waved as a huge commercial ship passed us, the first we have come across so far. She came from the other direction, and had been held back especially for us by the lockkeepers, so we would not all arrive at the lock at the same time.

By now Anna has come out of her shell and has found a quiet spot on deck, still wrapped up in her blanket. This is the first time she has ever set foot on a

Sobering to think that these locks were dug by hand

sailing boat. Only two weeks ago she turned seventeen and passed her school exams. There is a lot going on in her mind, as before long she is expected to go to Israel. Already studying Hebrew, she is hoping to become good enough to pass the entrance exam for the university in Haifa. I have never asked her why she is going all the way to Israel to study! Anna is a clever girl, and perhaps she has a better chance for higher education in Israel than in Russia. It is not nice for her to have to leave her parents, brother and friends behind. Vladimir, who is feeling very responsible for her, came round this morning to hand her his warm coat. Luckily there is no need as our cupboards are full of them. Every evening, after we have finally made a landfall, he and Anna usually go for a walk. Yesterday it was in search of edible mushrooms in the snake-infested surroundings. Seeing we had run out of bread, Elsbeth, who makes her own daily, gave us each a slice, together with some of their newly caught fish.

At the moment we are passing a tower along the shore, it is the only building left from a village that was flooded when the gates of the locks were put in. The village that was, is underneath us at this very moment. Just beyond lock number seven we stopped along a quayside, in the middle of nowhere. Whilst the skippers and crew searched the area for shops, I stayed behind and was

Facilities were in disrepair. This was the jetty at one of our overnight stops

handed a wild mushroom by three young girls. I think the word had spread that if they give you something they get something in return. I gladly obliged, as we were well prepared and had a bag full of gifts especially for occasions such as this. In the evening, around a campfire, I played the squeezebox, and Vladimir, Anna, and a local man who had joined us with his guitar, entertained us with Russian folk songs.

Me on the squeezebox, accompanying Alan's hornpipe

Anna, Vladimir and Vassiliev our pilot singing by the campfire

Drama in the Lock

2nd July, 2000

In order to organise my day I was up at 6am and by ten we were on our way to lock number eighteen. Really lock number thirty-six, as they are all double ones. One more lock after this and we will have reached the White Sea. Having arrived at the lock in the pouring rain, we were told that we would have to wait for three or four hours once inside. Willem's very quiet voice warned us over the VHF not to take any pictures, as the bridge just outside the lock gates was of military importance. Luckily I had heard this, but not Ray on *Babaji*, it seemed, who was seen snapping away by Willem and our pilot. Word came back to hide our cameras and films, as there was a possibility that the KGB would be around to confiscate them. Frantically I hid our rolls of film and searched for our disposable cameras. If they wanted to take anything, they could certainly take those. Luck was with us, as it never came to anything. After lunch Gordon, for once not having to fix anything, worked on planning our route for the White Sea. When we have rounded North Cape we will be free, free like the birds.

One side of the lock gates had been open, but now suddenly they are shut and we are locked in. We shall see what happens next. The central heating is on and we are watching a Russian cartoon on television. Our wet gear is decorating the cockpit. They could keep us here for days if they wanted, but we have Vladimir, Anna, and a pilot with us, which is very helpful.

It has just been announced that our secret bridge will open in about one hour's time. I will believe it when I see it. Anna, content with her blanket, has finally agreed to wear one of our warm coats, but not until she was told to do so by Alan on *Nomad*.

Suddenly the lock gates started to open, together with the bridge. A Russian, looking down on us in the locks, was shouting and making a lot of noise. Hating conflict of any kind, I decided to stay down below and not get involved. But I had to, as *Nomad* was in serious trouble. Our Russian, very drunk and excited at seeing the foreign yachts, had taken off his coat and launched himself ten metres down into the freezing cold water. He landed flat on his back, in a lock, a predicament nobody could hope to get out of alive. He must have hurt himself badly, but in spite of that managed to swim to *Nomad*'s stern, where he asked for vodka and cigarettes. Alan, staying calm, got hold of the VHF and asked Vladimir on *Spirit* for advice. Vladimir in no uncertain terms instructed Alan not to let him on board, and told him to stamp on the man's fingers should he try. By now, the boats had all let go of their mooring lines and were slowly moving towards the bridge. Knowing full well that our Russian would drown if not helped, Alan ignored Vladimir's instructions and took him on board. Vladimir was livid and shouted on the VHF for Alan to obey. Suddenly the casualty, having noticed that he had lost his passport in the water, pushed Brenda aside and, with a cry of despair, jumped in again. The timing of this could not have been worse. Once Brenda had managed to regain her balance and find her place behind the steering wheel it was too late. The wind had pushed *Nomad* sideways across the lock. In the meantime our Russian, having retrieved his passport, had managed to grab their large inflatable fender. But Brenda, who couldn't see over the side, did not know where he was. With horror we watched her desperate attempt to straighten up *Nomad* and regain some sort of control. But she could not help but crash into the side of the lock, crushing the man in the process. All of us held our breath, as we watched him hanging by one hand from their huge inflatable fender. His eyes were closed and he was injured and hypothermic.

By this time Brenda had managed to manoeuvre *Nomad* alongside *Fereale*, and just as I was about to board *Nomad* Colin jumped across instead. Together, they managed to heave the casualty on board, where he was given a hot drink and a warm coat. Grateful to have been saved, he told Colin, who was trying to keep the shivering man warm, that he loved him. Brenda thought this was funny and warned Colin about Aids, after which the humour was restored.

Vladimir, however, was not content with the situation and asked to speak to our casualty over the VHF. An impossible task, as he was either unwilling or unable. But he knew very well what his fate was going to be; something that had been made quite clear to him over the VHF. This time it was Anna on board *Fereale* who was targeted to speak to the casualty. This made Gordon furious and in a harsh voice he told her to tell Vladimir that it was God's will that we saved the man. Whether Vladimir was able to see the situation from the front of the fleet or not, anyone could see that this man was not going to survive if left behind. At last Alan was given a second option, that of taking the man to the nearest point where he could be handed over to the police. The latter was chosen, and in convoy we moved underneath and past our infamous bridge to the nearest dock in Belomorsk. Our Russian, very scared by now, unsuccessfully tried to throw his newly retrieved passport back into the water. But Colin caught it just in time and zipped it safely in the man's pocket. He felt bad, not knowing if he had done the right thing, and whether he would be better off with or without it. The police, who were waiting, asked Brenda and Alan many questions. Whether they wanted compensation for the damage caused to their boat, for instance. Still trying to save the man from even more hardship, they said there was no damage, and that it had all been an accident. That he had fallen into the lock and not jumped.

It was a sad moment when we watched him being taken away. Vladimir told me that he would be given lashings for what he had done, and go to prison. Poor man. He was in no state to be beaten—already injured and suffering from hypothermia. I was confused and shocked, that something so innocent looking can turn into something so serious. Vladimir told me whilst on the way to a local shop that this is a dangerous place. On any trip in the future, he said, he would lay down the rules and people were to obey him or else! I have strong feelings about it all and have to restrain myself from writing them down.

In the shop I managed to buy two loaves, funny-looking biscuits, tomatoes and beer. We were the first foreigners most people here had ever seen. It became apparent that we would be staying in this dock for one more day, and that diesel would be made available to us. Soon an antiquated van arrived, and all of us except *Spirit* filled up our tanks. In the most complicated way, using a large handle, the diesel was hand-pumped from rusty oil drums into dirty-looking jerry cans. Clean or not, Gordon filtered and filtered again, before the diesel was poured into our tanks. We had no choice, as the last time we had tanked up was in Petrozavodsk. Not until we arrived in Vardø did someone tell us that we should have specifically asked for Finnish diesel.

The lock incident has badly affected Anna, and I caught her crying in the saloon. Understanding what she is going through, I made her comfortable on the sofa with her blanket. There is a meeting going on with some of the skippers in our cockpit. They are discussing the White Sea, and whether or not we should stay together. Colin is worried about getting to Murmansk in time for his flight home, and so are many others. Ray is concerned that we won't have a Russian speaker on board anymore, once in the White Sea. One of his crew, desperate to jump ship, has found sanctuary on *Spirit* as far as Murmansk. There are also concerns about money needed for the various services.

The Russian authorities want to know our potential stopovers. We will have to stick to their rigid plans, and make sure that we arrive earlier rather than later in Murmansk. A sudden meeting was called in the harbour master's office, where charts were checked and tide tables discussed. Ships papers and crew lists had to be shown. Our pilot has to inform the Russian authorities along the borders of the White Sea and Barents Sea of our plans. The main thing is that soon we will be free of needing a pilot. Like a dog about to be let off its lead, *Spirit* informed us that she will join us as far as the Solovetsky Islands, after which she intends to go her own way. Also *Babaji*, who has always been independent, will go her own way. Ray's wish is to venture further onwards to uncharted areas, something we are not keen to do. *Nomad*, *Fereale* and *Endring* plan to remain in contact. We hope to at least stay within VHF range or relay, whilst in Russian waters. I quietly escaped to my cabin, leaving Vladimir and Anna to try to find a telephone somewhere.

3rd July, 2000
To our surprise Anna left us this morning. I had told Vladimir that the lock incident had upset her, which shocked him. It was best she went back home, he said, wanting to protect her from any further incidents. Sadly we watched her pack her few belongings, before giving her some food for the long train journey to St Petersburg. Both of us felt emotional and wondered if we would ever see each other again.

Next on the agenda was a guided tour of the local maritime museum, which looked like a huge container. Gordon was unable to join us since he had lots of things to do, like preparing *Fereale* for the White Sea. A lady in Karelian costume showed us around, and Vladimir was our translator. A beautiful painting of a saint, dating back to 1634, caught my eye. It had been saved from the fires during the revolution. I was impressed, but had difficulty understanding what was said. An old bus was waiting outside and took us to see the White

Sea carvings. About two thousand images have been discovered near Belomorsk, some six thousand years old. Carved on gentle sloping rocks, we saw hunting scenes of elk, whales and bears, and boats with dozens of oarsmen. Vladimir, together with our Russian lady guide, explained the meaning of the hunting scene to us. On our

Rock carvings near Belomorsk

Belomorsk graveyard

way back to Belomorsk the bus stopped at an open market, where we stocked up on food. We partied in the evening as, not only had Anna left us, Vladimir and the pilot were also leaving.

5th July, 2000
One more lock to go, the lock that is to take us to the White Sea and beyond. As we left, some Russians waved at us and gave us the thumbs up. Once in the White Sea, Gordon felt free—the freedom of being back in the open sea. Not me, however; I won't feel free until we have reached Norway. I am sure that the lock incident has a lot to do with it. The wind is dead on the nose, which makes it impossible for us to sail. We seem to have a problem with the compass on our mast, which is not corresponding with the steering compass in the cockpit. Because of this, we can't use the autopilot and will have to steer by hand. Perhaps it is due to the magnetic field of the earth underneath us, which is not the same around here. Maybe there is a deposit of iron ore under the seabed, which is disrupting things. Not until later in our journey did we discover that sticky bearings were the cause.

We are approaching the Solovetsky Islands, situated in the south-western part of the White Sea. Solovetsky is the central island in the archipelago and has one of the largest monasteries in the world, dating back to 1600. In the distance we can see the giant walls of the monastery, built from boulders weighing many tons. The White Sea, famous for its fog, is giving us an easy time today and we have clear visibility. Navigation is tense, though, as some islands are not marked on the chart, and the cardinal buoys that are marked are nowhere to be seen. *Spirit*, *Nomad* and *Fereale* have all slowed down since, for a while, all three boats were lost. Having found the leading lights at last, we arrived safely and moored up along the quayside of Ostrov Solovetsky. *Endring* and *Babaji*, who are unable to carry as much diesel as us, are using nothing but their sails. It did not take long before Gordon, Colin and Willem were off to explore the area. I stayed behind to cook the dinner and guard *Fereale*. Everyone is keen to find a place to eat tonight; only Gordon is able to understand why I refuse to leave *Fereale* unattended. There are a lot of curious youngsters about who feel the need to climb on board. It is innocent enough, but having once caught a burglar out, I didn't really want it to happen again. For the time being I am happy with my diary and some peace and quiet.

Our first sight of Solovetsky

The Monastery at Solovetsky at the height of summer

Throughout the Stalin era the monastery functioned as a prison camp, one of the infamous gulags. After the communist revolution Solovetsky became the victim of terrible massacres. This particular monastery, built like a fortress, became a concentration camp in which thousands of people died. It is only now, after the fall of the Communist regime, that the church bells are ringing once more. The main island has about fourteen hundred inhabitants, most of whom are illiterate. Some work in the monastery, the museum, or on the various projects on the island. In winter there is round-the-clock polar darkness. More than fifty percent of the men spend their time in a drunken state, with nothing else to do. Students all the way from Moscow come here to help with the restoration work, in the two or three months of summer. A few of those able to speak English came to see me, asking if they could have a lift to the other side. They had many questions, and were amazed to learn that we had come all the way from Holland. It is strange to think that we have not yet reached the halfway mark.

At eight in the evening an official came to the boats, asking for crew lists and clearance papers. They had been expecting us, he gestured. Tomorrow, we should get our papers back. Colin is having a wonderful time. He is clearly

An evening fishing at Solovetsky

on holiday, a feeling that we should be sharing but don't. I am sure that this is because of the responsibility that we are carrying, that of getting *Fereale* safely through Russia. Everyday Gordon still finds water at the bottom of our day tank. So far we have been lucky, and he has managed to drain it off before it's had a chance to reach the engine. In the evening *Endring* arrived, and André is discussing with Gordon where to look for sperm whales off the coast of Andenes, in Norway. André is a marine biologist and worked there for a few years. It is great fun talking about the things we really love to see and do.

6th July, 2000
At about 2am, when both of us were fast asleep, I heard knocking on the boat. Confused, I got up and found a young man in our cockpit trying to sell me a carved wooden spoon. I was touched but also shocked at the fact that he had managed to get on board unnoticed. I did not feel like hunting for a purse at two in the morning and declined buying the spoon, only to watch him climb on board *Spirit of Aeolus* next, with poor Willem about to get the same surprise. Part of me wants to get out of Russia and part of me wants to stay. I would love to have the time without other pressures to get to know the people here and their culture, and not to have to stick to these rigid timetables.

It is morning now and last night's wind has finally calmed down. It has been a cold night and, even with the heating on, Gordon was shivering. I am looking out over the monastery, so beautiful with its onion-topped church towers, and am more ready now for what today will bring us. Elsbeth and I went shopping and managed to buy some solid bread, cheese of a kind, butter, Mars Bars and tinned bear meat. Most houses here do not have a water supply, and we watched women carrying their buckets to and fro. We saw one such place where they go, just a tap by the side of the road with a couple of wooden benches. Who knows, these people may be very happy living this way. I would love to be a fly on the wall in one of their houses, to see how they cope during their severe winters and to learn from *them*, instead of the other way around. We have little to teach them, as they can cope with life better than any of us. Content with the food we were able to acquire we trotted back to the boats, meeting one of *Babaji*'s crew on the way, doing his hand-washing in a stream.

Gordon is twitchy about getting *Fereale*'s papers back. Together with Colin he has gone in search of the harbour master, as tonight we will depart on the epic voyage to Murmansk. With his phrase book ever at-the-ready, Colin approached the locals and asked for directions. With blank looks on their faces they pointed in the direction of a most unlikely-looking shack. Deciding to give that one a miss, Colin and Gordon eventually ended up at the local town hall a mile or so up the road. There they found the town mayor who, to their delight, spoke English. They were whisked off in his jeep and taken to the same unlikely-looking shack that had been pointed out to them by the locals in the first place! Inside, there was a wood stove burning in the centre and, in what must have been the kitchen,

Gordon in search of the harbour office, Solovetsky

a bucket on the floor surrounded by dishes. Having been taken by surprise our man got out of his bunk and hurriedly put on a shirt. Even the television was quickly switched on in their honour. It was not long before the necessary papers had been handed over, and both men were back on board.

While our mosquito coils keep the flies at bay in the saloon, outside the deck is covered by millions of the nasty beasts. The wind, normally predominantly from the north, for once has turned south. We must leave soon and make the most of this wind as we have four or five days of non-stop sailing ahead of us.

After a rest, and with plenty of food inside us, we said goodbye to the rest of the fleet. *Fereale*, being one of the slower boats under sail, did well to be the first to leave. It was Brenda and Alan who, at ten in the evening, helped cast off our lines and waved us goodbye whilst blowing the foghorn. We also managed to catch a glimpse of Willem at the end of the pier. Our adventure has really started now, after the chaos of the inland waterways. No longer do we have to play the game of follow my leader.

The White Sea

7th July, 2000

It is 3am and already the sun is rising in the sky, rising from just above the horizon since it never sets. As there is hardly any wind, we are forced to motor sail. The three of us are able to get plenty of rest. Not long now until we will have reached the Arctic Circle. The Solovetsky Islands have disappeared out of sight and we are completely on our own. Now and again we hear Russian voices on the VHF, perhaps they are asking us something. The various authorities must have been informed by now that the five boats have left Solovetsky, and they must have heard us speak to the other boats over the VHF. We are ignoring them for the moment and are concentrating on crossing over to the Kola Peninsula, under strict instructions not to stop anywhere along that coast. The Kola Peninsula is a barren place, which separates the White Sea from the Arctic Ocean. Sadly I had to disturb Gordon's peace when I noticed that our new starter battery was overcharging. A problem he soon managed to solve, which was a weight off my mind.

It is now late in the afternoon and Gordon is depressed, having found yet more water at the bottom of our day tank and a leaking exhaust. Quickly he switched off our engine, and with that everything electronic. Looking at the positive side, my fridge is getting its first defrost and clean since Holland! To gain some speed we hoisted our spinnaker, only to have to drop it again a couple of hours later owing to a change of course. To our delight, we heard first Alan and then André over the VHF, as the two boats were about to catch us up.

8th July, 2000

It has been a funny night with dense fog, interspersed with the strangest cloud formations; a phenomenon we have never seen before. The White Sea, famous for its fog, is treating us kindly. Now with the sun high in the sky we are fighting a strong current, as all of the White Sea goes in and out of this ten-mile bottleneck. I am scanning the coastline with my binoculars and admit to feeling a little scared. Everything looks so bleak and uninviting and I have somehow convinced myself that any ship we might come across will be our enemy. Totally ridiculous of course, but in my generation we were brought up to fear Russia. One of the reasons for this trip is to break through that mentality. I would have been fine had it not been for the lock incident. The lashings our man received seem to fit my view of this forbidding coastline. For the time being, anyway, my confidence has vanished. There is some comfort, however, as *Nomad* has appeared on the horizon. Brenda and Alan have told us that, should the need arise due to water in our diesel, they would tow us all the way around the North Cape. That is, of course, in the unlikely event of no wind.

Things are going well. Our crew, Colin, has a very easy-going nature and I wonder if there is anything at all that can fluster him. A little while ago we heard André from the Norwegian boat, *Endring*, talking to *Spirit*, both still out of sight and astern of us. We could not hear *Spirit*'s answer but relayed back to *Nomad*, some way ahead, that there was contact at least. The first thing we do is to give each other our positions and check them on the chart. The only boat we do not have a position for is *Babaji*, but we are not expecting Ray to get in touch. We are confused as to the reason why *Spirit of Aeolus*, the fastest boat in the fleet, is lagging behind. Soon *Endring* relayed back, to tell us that for some time now *Spirit*'s crew have been hearing mysterious noises coming from their engine room! Concerned about this they have slowed down and are taking it easy.

It is 10pm and instead of a choppy sea there is a huge swell. We have now reached the polar circle and the current is sweeping us through the bottleneck at a speed of 9.6 knots. In two hours' time, when the tide changes, we will need to get closer to the shore to dodge the counter current. The huge swell and the ripples in the water caused by the current constantly amaze me. Nowadays the concern over the Kola Peninsula is not over the military and submarine stations along the shore, but of the nuclear waste that has been dumped here. Although it is not evident, we are sailing over the most poisoned spot on earth.

The Barents Sea

By now the sun is so far north that it barely touches the horizon before it rises once more.

Suddenly I became excited, but nervous at the same time. Approaching *Fereale* was a sperm whale! As he came closer to the boat his size became more evident. He came so close that I could have touched him. I should have called Colin and Gordon who were sleeping, but did not. I should have taken a picture, but did not. Looking to port I noticed another two going in the opposite direction. It amazed me that *Fereale* had not collided with him and I started to concentrate even harder on what was ahead of me, in case there were more. When I dared look astern of me my friends had vanished, and I had missed their spectacular dive to the bottom of the sea. Excitedly I called up *Nomad* on the VHF, whose mast I could still see in the distance, and told Brenda what I had seen. I also said that I was on my own and that the men were fast asleep. Being just that little bit too far away she didn't hear my mention of the whales, just the bit about me being on my own. "You poor thing," she said, "and so alone!" This confused me even more, as I knew she would have been excited for me. Gordon, when awake, took out our whale book, and together we read what we could about them. The sperm whale is the strangest of all the great whales. A huge animal, that likes to think that he is a submarine.

It is bitterly cold outside and nearly 1am. Time to get the polar gloves out of hiding and wake up Colin, as hand steering and plotting positions are difficult in this swell. Dressed up in foul weather gear he took over from me in the freezing cold, and I watched the hot chocolate in his hands create steam around his face. At last I was able to concentrate solely on navigation. *Nomad* has disappeared out of sight and has taken an inner route, one that our pilot had advised us to take. It goes through a prohibited area and Gordon, not trusting our pilot, decided not to follow suit. We are now in the Barents Sea, and have another hundred and twenty miles to go to Murmansk. The sea is mountainous and the waves have steep walls and deep valleys. Whilst I was preparing breakfast I heard a sudden shout coming from the cockpit. This time it was Colin who had spotted a whale, and a white one at that—a beluga.

We are all feeling seasick and cooking the evening meal was not an easy task. The coastline has changed dramatically and looks rugged, with last year's snow still visible. Sailing at the moment is tedious and tiring.

9th July, 2000
At 9am it was time for Gordon and me to reef our main and take down the jib, a struggle in the ever-increasing wind. A calm soon descended over us, as *Fereale* was once more under control. Sadly, Gordon had forgotten to put

Gordon, arctic foredeck hand

on his gloves during our battle and all of his fingers had been exposed to the freezing temperature of the water. In agony he returned to the cockpit with near frostbitten hands where, with the help of our lined fishermen's gloves, his fingers slowly thawed out. Whilst reefing our main he had discovered that the webbing tape holding the top slider on the mainsail was torn, and that the gate on the track had broken. From now on it was 'Onwards Christian Soldiers', under staysail only. It is bleak, cold and forbidding, and still another three hours to go before we enter the fjord that leads to Murmansk. Time to call the local coastal station to inform them of our approximate time of arrival, and give them our call sign and position. All of this was acknowledged with a lot of Russian chatter, none of which we understood. On the chart we can see that the area is scattered with shipwrecks. Intensely we scan the surface for masts, which apparently still protrude above the waterline. From inside I watched Colin being christened by a huge wave, and think he will have years of yarns to tell when he gets back home. It is impossible to do anything down below, and I hear the seawater gurgling in the drain of our sink. It is time to shut its seacock.

Colin on watch, Barents Sea

Colin off watch, Barents Sea

Murmansk

At last we have turned into the estuary, and we have literally sailed off the chart. I must admit that I don't mind being down below, and that Colin and Gordon are taking charge. There is plenty to do, and I need to tidy up the damp mess. Gordon, who saw a boat ahead of us, is wondering if it could possibly be a pilot boat and has decided to follow. In poor visibility, but in the shelter from the mainland, we motor in the strong current towards Murmansk, with another twenty miles to go.

Despite its northerly location the flow of the warm Atlantic Gulf Stream keeps this harbour and many others permanently ice-free in winter. At the entrance of the estuary there is a major nuclear submarine station. We were to meet one of these submarines later in our travels, whilst still in Russia and on our way to the North Cape. Both men, having had a stiff drink by now, are in a good mood, nevertheless envious of me in the warmth down below. On the VHF we can hear Russian being spoken, and recognise the word 'yachts', but little else. We hope that Brenda and Alan on *Nomad* have arrived safely, and that *Endring*, the smallest boat in the fleet, is OK. *Spirit* is in sight and is slowly overtaking us, her crew still mystified by the strange sounds coming from their engine room.

We have been at sea now for four days and four nights and are about a hundred and fifty miles north of the Arctic Circle. The shoreline seems to be used to house old sunken ships, once recovered from the depths of the sea. Gordon is taking a nap, and Colin has taken over watch. I have to restrain myself from going into the cockpit, as I don't want to interrupt his thoughts.

I am happy and content down below and now and again take a picture from our porthole; scared that should I do this from the cockpit I could possibly be arrested.

Suddenly we saw *Nomad*, together with *Spirit*, safely moored alongside and followed suit. Relieved to have arrived at last, we came alongside *Nomad*. Climbing ashore to secure a line, I was stopped by two officials in green coats. They thought I was leaving the boat, but with sign language I soon made it clear I was not going anywhere. Brenda and Alan, having arrived quite a few hours ahead of us, were able to give some good advice on what to expect next.

Soon five officials boarded *Fereale*. Our plan had been not to invite them down below, but to deal with the formalities from the table in our cockpit. Unbeknown to me one official had sneaked down below via the aft hatch,

where he was confronted by Colin. Whilst Colin kept a close eye on him, the officer proceeded to look in every cupboard for a possible stowaway. One of the officials was a woman, and the only English-speaking person there, who informed us that she was going to be our agent. We were rather surprised at this, as none of us were aware that we needed one, and were wary of what it would cost. She informed us that everything had gone wrong on our way to Murmansk. They had not expected us to arrive for at least another two days! We told her that at first

Our berth in Murmansk

we had little wind, after which we had a lot and went faster than expected. Not happy with that, she continued to say that we should have reported at every coastal station we passed on our way and given our call sign. "We did," we said, "but never received a reply." "If these were communist times," she said, "you would have been in serious trouble." We felt like telling her that if these were communist times we would have never undertaken this trip in the first place.

Nuclear icebreaker

Cold war warrior, Murmansk

Apparently the last time they saw a foreign yacht in Murmansk was back in 1990, ten years ago. In St Petersburg the officials are more used to seeing foreign yachts and a ship's agent was not required. But here the officials seemed to be following big ship procedures and we had obviously sailed in unaware of this. Our passports and crew lists were checked, along with what food we carried and how much money. They were concerned about *Endring* who had not arrived yet, and so were we. Michou, a kind young Russian seaman whom we had met before, came to our rescue. He had flown into Murmansk to join *Endring* to sail to Kirkenes in Norway. The intention was that he would meet up with a German boat there and guide her all the way back through Russia to the Gulf of Finland! Michou was a great help as he spoke English and ironed out any difficulties we might have had.

Colin, much to his surprise, had managed to reach his wife, Diane, in England on his mobile. She, in turn, would relay news of our safe arrival in

Welcome to officialdom, Murmansk

Formalities can be so boring!

Murmansk to our children. Colin's main concern was how to pay for his flight back to England, one that had been booked in advance. Our lady agent was very helpful, but informed him that in order to get his exit stamp he would need to book into a local hotel. When it was time to go to bed *Endring* finally arrived. Never before had we seen André so tired. We were to discover why the following day.

10th July, 2000

The first job after breakfast was for Gordon to repair our mainsail. In the meantime all the ladies went shopping at the local market, with two English-speaking Russians summoned by Michou. In two cars, and with just enough space for Colin, Alan and Willem as our guardians, we set off. We managed to get everything we needed; vegetables, bread, eggs, and even chicken. Returning to *Fereale* I found Gordon on board *Endring*, who had serious problems! On their way to Murmansk their steering wheel had jammed. Barely able to turn it, they had only just managed to enter the harbour, where it had seized completely. Gordon, wanting to help, impressed André by being able to produce his *Mechanical and Electrical Manual*, which had detailed drawings of

Endring's steerage system. Together they took the wheel apart and drilled out the brake, after which oil was poured into the steerage column. But as well as this problem they had yet another. They had been informed that they were only allowed to stay in Murmansk for twenty-four hours. It seemed that one of their crew had a visa that expired the day they arrived, a mistake made by the authorities when he applied, and one too late to rectify before their departure.

All during our passage to Murmansk I wished that our orange storm sail had been hanked onto the mast. There is a track especially designed for this sail on the mast. Not wanting to be caught out again, I began digging it out of hiding. Even if we didn't need to use it, at least it would be there ready and waiting.

All of us were horrified when we learned that our agent was going to charge each boat $350, a fee that we each had to pay if we were to get our exit stamp. This was a ridiculous amount of money of course, and money none of us were prepared to pay. Since *Endring* and her crew were to be the first to leave, and had no more than $50 at their disposal, we were intrigued to see how the matter would be resolved.

Major crew changes were taking place on *Spirit of Aeolus*. Always a well-crewed yacht, people came and went, but now Elsbeth was leaving also. Since Holland she had suffered a badly ulcerated leg, and was in need of urgent treatment. She will be flying to Hammerfest in Norway, where it had been arranged for her to go to hospital. I feel sorry for her, as she will have to miss the North Cape. On top of that, her shoulder keeps popping out of its socket. Willem keeps putting it back in. This is OK if he is around, but if not it is absolutely awful, as most friends or strangers are unwilling or unable to handle such a problem. Most of the time she is well bandaged up and wears a corset. The idea is that *Spirit of Aeolus* will pick her up in Hammerfest after having rounded the North Cape.

Gordon, who left André to put his steering column back together, was immediately summoned by Willem for yet another problem. Even Brenda and Alan, whom I visited, were quietly suffering. They also needed Gordon but were too embarrassed to ask, knowing how busy he was. But we were all there to help each other, after all, and for Gordon to work on someone else's problem was easier than working on his own. Quite proud of my man, I watched as he managed to solve their problems also. Now it was time to see to *Fereale*, with minor problems like another hole in the exhaust, a black engine room, and water in the diesel! We needed to find someone to help us this time, someone who could weld a particular part of our exhaust. But first it had to be unbolted and taken out. Soon Gordon disappeared with an agent in search of an engineer. Colin, in the meantime, had made a start on cleaning the engine room, an absolutely filthy task.

Colin kindly wants to take us out for a meal tomorrow, as it will be his last night on board. The authorities have relented and have decided to let him stay his last night with us after all. We have to thank our boat stamp for this, as it seemed to impress them. Any boat that has not got one is frowned upon. At last I was persuaded to join, although once again I was worrying about leaving our boat unattended. Brenda and Alan will also join us, all of them determined to treat both Gordon and me. But first we had to say goodbye to *Endring*. André had told us that he had to produce a list with all the safety equipment carried on board. I quickly went down below and prepared one too, just in case.

At 8pm André was still struggling to put his steering column together. Gordon offered to lend a hand as time was marching on. Everything was only just put back together when the officials boarded to give *Endring* the all clear. They seemed to stay for ages, but Michou was also there, no doubt his influence would be of great help. To our surprise we had managed to get a weather forecast on our Navtex from Archangel. The first one in ages, and one I was keen to give to André before he left. With a piece of paper in my hand, I tried to board *Endring*, but was stopped in my tracks. She had been cleared, and nobody was to board her. Using sign language, I managed to persuade one of the guards to pass on my note. All of us were delighted when we heard that the fees had been dropped from $350 per boat to $30 a day. For *Endring*, having been in Murmansk for only one day, this was not bad. We watched André and his tired crew leave, and silently prayed that his steering column would cause no further problems.

During our visit to Kizhi Island I was stung by a fly on both eyelids. It is quite nasty and has left me with blurred vision ever since. I shall have to monitor this carefully, as it is a great nuisance!

Murmansk is our halfway mark and it won't be long before we will be on or our way. Another hundred miles to go, and we will have reached Norway, with a time difference of two hours.

11th July, 2000

Up late for a change, but straight into work as usual. To our delight we noticed that *Babaji* had arrived in the middle of the night. This time it was she who had to endure official procedures, but in the early morning hours instead. I feel apprehensive, as we are leaving tomorrow and there is a strong wind blowing. Our engine room is still black, and the leak in our exhaust has not yet been fixed. Colin is packing his bags in preparation for his flight back home. Looking for some comfort, I visited Brenda and Alan. Always welcoming, they let me have a little weep, gave me some wine, and positioned me on their best bunk surrounded by cushions. I worry about Gordon, as there seem to be so many things that I can't help him with; jobs that only an engineering mind can solve. Brenda and Alan understand my concerns but have problems of their own. Feeling a lot better I returned to *Fereale* where I took on the job of restocking our cupboards with food found in the most inaccessible places. Dear Gordon, who saw I was down, took the time to show me on the charts how close to Norway we really were.

Alan, who can't start *Nomad*'s engine, has summoned a Russian engineer. He does not want to ask Gordon, who is heavily involved in other problems. A job he could have easily helped him with, though. Nearly 9pm and a repaired but still suspect-looking exhaust was fitted back in place. Unfortunately, one of the four screws that holds it in place has lost its thread. Not having the correct tap for that, we have no alternative but to leave it as it is and hope that no poisonous gases will escape. After a quick tidy and clean up the five of us were on our way to a local restaurant, surprisingly hidden on the premises. There we enjoyed a wonderful dinner with background music from a local band. Willem, Elsbeth and their newly arrived crew were dining there also, but in a different room together with the press. During the day Colin had arranged for a taxi, one that was to come at 6am and take him to the airport. We shall miss his company and hope that he has had a good time. Elsbeth, too, will be leaving in the morning. She will be taking a bus to Kirkenes followed by a flight to Hammerfest.

12th July, 2000

I woke Colin at 5am and made him breakfast; fried eggs on toast and a strong cup of tea. Together with Brenda and Alan, amazingly fresh so early in the morning, we waved as the taxi drove him away. It feels strange but also nice, as for the first time in four weeks we are on our own again. Gordon, hardly daring to stick his head out of the cabin, was called to help solve a problem on *Spirit*. However much we want to help, it leaves us with no time to think about how to solve our own issues. The weather has changed for the better, thank goodness, and we are hoping that it will stay this way for our departure tomorrow. At 1pm Gordon at last had time to go for a walk. He has not been away from the boat at all since our arrival in Murmansk. But no such luck. The police at the gate stopped him and asked for his passport and papers. Any desire for him to see anything of Russia has been totally destroyed by all the hassle and bureaucracy. Next I watched as Alan tried to stop our lady agent from climbing over his boat towards *Fereale*. He did not like the high heels she was wearing, although he did not mind the short skirt. He asked her kindly to take her shoes off, something she flatly refused to do. Furious, he looked on as she managed to get her own way. However sorry I felt for Alan, I was slightly amused.

Once she had reached our cockpit, she told us the bad news. She had heard that *Endring* was in trouble at the end of the fjord. Could it have something to do with the steering, Gordon wondered, the one that he had repaired? We listened to what else she had to say and heard that they had managed to anchor somewhere in the fjord. We all know that once any of us have been cleared we are not allowed to enter any port till Norway. Our only consolation was that the coastguard was obviously aware of the situation. But that was not everything. She went on to explain that the river leading to the sea was going to close to all traffic; something the military do quite frequently, apparently, to allow for naval exercises. They wanted to clear us today, this afternoon, and watch us leave as soon as possible. Gordon did not believe any of it and was convinced that it was all planned. He told her, tongue in cheek, that we could not leave till 5am the following morning. The tide would be right then, he said, and continued to bargain for a discount, if they wanted to clear us any sooner. With that message in her mind, she left *Fereale*. The most important thing on our minds was *Endring*, and soon Gordon, Alan and Willem gathered on *Spirit of Aeolus* to prepare a plan of rescue. None of us had received our clearance papers. If we managed to find *Endring* in the morning, which of us would tow her round the North Cape? What if the steering gear, assuming that that was the problem, could not be repaired?

Back she came again, our lady agent, but this time with the news that the three boats would be cleared at 4am. Gordon's bargaining had obviously helped!

<table>
<tr><td>C C C P</td><td>U S S R</td></tr>
<tr><td>МУРМАНСКОЕ</td><td>MURMANSK</td></tr>
<tr><td>ГЛАВНОЕ</td><td>MAIN</td></tr>
<tr><td>МОРСКОЕ</td><td>MARITIME</td></tr>
<tr><td>АГЕНТСТВО</td><td>AGENCY</td></tr>
<tr><td>«ИНФЛОТ»</td><td>«INFLOT»</td></tr>
</table>

Адрес:
CCCP, 183038, Мурманск
Портовый пр., 19
Телегр: ИНФЛОТ МУРМАНСК
Телекс: 196
Телефон: 25-197, 25-666,

Address,
19, Portovy Proezd
Murmansk, 183038/USSR
Cables: INFLOT MURMANSK
Telex: 196
Tel. 25-197, 25-666,

Our ref: _____

MURMANSK SHIPPING AGENCY "INFLOT", RUSSIA

VOUCHER

THE *13* TH OF JULY, 2000   M/V " *Fereale* "   (*Holland*)
                                          (Name)   (flag)

FOR PORT CLEARANCE:

USD 100=00 (ONE HUNDRED US DOLLARS)

PAID IN CASH.

MASTER *Campbell*
            (signature)

AGENT _____
            (signature)

Clearance papers, Murmansk

Goodbye to Russia

4am. Time to be cleared but still no sign of customs. Gordon is making use of his time by putting waypoints into the GPS. Alan's daughter, who is a helicopter pilot, had warned her dad that at 70° north our GPSs might have a problem finding the satellites. We shall have to take that as it comes.

A miracle has happened and both *Spirit* and *Fereale* were cleared by 5am. The officials kept on referring to Gordon as 'Captain', and it was hard for him to keep a straight face. Once again our boat stamp proved to be of major importance. They also came to tell us that *Endring* had arrived in Norway! This was wonderful news, but what had happened in the fjord? Not until we reached Norway did we find out the real reason for André's problems. Whilst handling the sails and running the engine at the same time, one of the jib sheets had wound itself around the prop of his engine. Unbeknown to André it had been trailing in the water. Michou, in a diving suit, had managed to untangle it. Gordon was much relieved that it had not been the steering gear after all that had been at fault.

One by one we left Murmansk, with no sign of the river being closed. We are both delighted, but our dear *Fereale* is absolutely filthy, having been in a commercial harbour for so long. So are we, come to think of it, as we still need to ration our water supply, last topped up in Lake Onega. Another twenty-four hours and we will have reached Vardø. The weather is good and there is little wind, only 5am and the sun is already beating down on us. We are committed now. Norway, here we come! Gordon asked me if I thought it had all been

121

worthwhile, and I replied that, yes, it has. Not many people experience what we have seen and done. Vladimir Yermakova, Anna's dad, had told us that it had been their aim to make all of us feel as comfortable as possible during our stay in Russia. Vladimir Gromov, Vladimir Ivankiv and Michou had faced many obstacles on the way, all of which were of a bureaucratic nature. I am sure that only they, like no one else, know how to handle such problems. We had been lucky, he said, and had been unaware of most. He also assured us that it was not material gain or profit that had governed them, but that it had been the spirit of friendship that had driven them in their quest. Of all of this I am convinced, as we have received nothing but kindness. Not only has it been a unique experience for us, but also for them.

It will take another four hours before we are out of the fjord, with *Spirit of Aeolus* for once not rushing out of sight. I managed to get a couple of hours of sleep and did not take over from Gordon until we were at sea. After a few hours into my watch I noticed something fast coming towards us. What was it? And what was happening? My legs turned to jelly. "Don't be so silly," I told myself and slapped my thigh. To my utter surprise I stopped shaking straight away and regained control. Gordon, having been alerted, poked his sleepy head out of the cockpit and told me in a quiet voice that it was a nuclear submarine that was approaching us at thirty knots. They must have wondered who the hell these boats were in their territory. As *Nomad*, *Spirit* and *Fereale* formed a triangle, with *Fereale* lagging behind, the submarine parked itself in front of us. Having thought I was about to round its stern I now seemed to be heading for its bow instead. Alarmed, Gordon, who seemed to know the difference, grabbed the wheel and only just managed to alter course in time. Soon little men with binoculars appeared from the conning tower from where we were observed. In fact, they circled each boat in turn, in order to read their names. Slowly I raised my hand and managed a little wave. We can only guess that they must have called Murmansk and inquired about us aliens, to see if we had cleared out properly, and where we had come from in the first place. The Russians on the submarine would never call us themselves, for security reasons. The coastguard did, however, and called us one by one by name, and asked for our position and destination. The submarine continued to hover around us for a while, after which she disappeared like a whale into the depth below. She is probably following us, making sure we don't turn right, instead of left.

We were checked out of Russia by one of the many Cold War warriors. Was it the Kursk?

Leaving Russia feels like leaving Qatar, where we lived for six months in 1995 to 1996. Neither are free societies. It is 4pm and with the wind on our tail we are motor sailing. In spite of a dubious exhaust Gordon refuses to switch off our engine until we have crossed the border of Russia. The first bit of land to starboard of us is Spitsbergen, far above the Arctic Circle in the north. It is funny to think that if we sailed there it would only take us a few days. We feel that our every move is being monitored and can hear Russian chatter coming from Channel 77. All I can say is that they must have very powerful transmitters, as we are virtually out of sight of land. *Nomad*, who called us a little while ago, was joking about a big whale and we feel that the Russians are discussing the likes of us this very moment. Once we have arrived in Vardø we will be home, in spite of having another two thousand nautical miles to go to Holland.

It is chilly and the wind is icy cold. I dread to think what the temperature of the water is like. Tonight we should be able to sleep a little longer, as the clocks go back two hours. Not long ago the Norwegian flag went up, and we celebrated our taste of freedom with a glass of whisky for Gordon and a gin and tonic for me. Both of us feel relieved. Sailing through Russia has taught us a lot, and all together we have come out of it as stronger people. A lot of hardship and also frustration has gone into *Fereale*'s preparations, but she is worth every bit and we will sail the seas with her any time. Finally, at 11pm, we enter Vardø, recognisable by its huge radar dome left over from the cold war. It points straight at Russia and is an early warning system. The Russians themselves have one that looks the same, but points at Vardø instead. The puffins that welcome us look like little black and white clowns with red noses, they are such comical birds. A rainbow is decorating the town and suddenly we see houses with paint on them again. Willem and Alan were there to take our lines after which we had the most peaceful sleep in a long time, in spite of being surrounded by noisy seagulls.

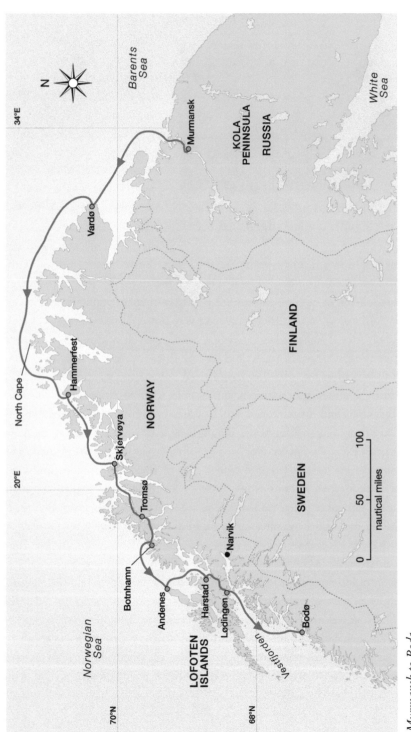

Murmansk to Bodø

Norway

14th July, 2000

Vardø, oh Vardø, how nice it is to feel free and to be welcomed into your lovely town where we can come and go as we please.

The sun is shining and I can't wait to get my bike out, something that has not happened since Finland. I can't wait to cycle to the nearest phone box and call our girls and Mum, to shop without hassle and to speak Norwegian. It is Saturday and the diesel stations in harbour are closing at lunchtime. We need to hurry, so as not to get stuck here for the weekend.

After finding a fishing vessel prepared to dispose of our dirty diesel, we tanked up with the clearest ever seen. The vessel had come from Kristiansund, all the way to Vardø to fish for shrimp. The skipper told us that crossing the North Cape was a matter of routine for them. "We often hire Russian crew," he said. "They are not prepared for the harsh conditions at sea and we have to kit them out with new waterproofs and clothes. When they come on board they have nothing, not even a toothbrush or comb." My heart, already warm towards the Norwegians, is warming even more. Gordon bought a kilo of freshly peeled shrimps from them—a treat for when we round the North Cape ourselves, the most northern part of Europe.

Spirit of Aeolus left some time ago, destination Hammerfest, some one hundred and ninety miles from here. There they will collect Elsbeth, having had the correct treatment for her ulcerated leg, we hope. Our destination is the same, but not until we have had a good rest. The white summer nights are lighter than I had expected and it is strange to still be able to sit in the cockpit at

Vardo

midnight and read a book. Here one can see the sun for twenty-four hours a day, from 14th May until 30th July. I have confused the midnight sun for the Northern lights in the past, a spectacle that can only be seen in wintertime. It would be nice if every day could last this long.

15th July, 2000
It is six o'clock in the morning and we are on our way. The weather is beautiful. We are in no rush, have no engine noise and are making five knots. *Nomad* left before us and is about three miles ahead. Gordon is tired and has gone down for a rest, whilst I am in my element watching the seagulls. They think we are a fishing boat and it is just wonderful to have their company. The eddies that obstruct our speed are caused by the Arctic current that flows past this coast, and the Atlantic current a little further out. In bad weather they can cause dangerous waves, but the weather is good to us and we are making the most of it. Somehow the Norwegian coastline does not frighten me like the Russian coastline did, although both are equally forbidding. Here we feel that, should we be in trouble, we are amongst friends. In Russia they still have a hangover from the communist times and it feels different somehow.

It is evening now and soon I shall make a special dinner to fill our hungry stomachs. Tomorrow sometime we will round the North Cape. We are saving our precious shrimps for the occasion, together with a bottle of champagne.

When I called up *Nomad* we were surprised that the answer came from Gamvik, where it seemed they, and *Spirit of Aeolus*, had stopped for the night. We, ourselves, are not going to stop but will continue on to Hammerfest. It is ten o'clock in the evening and I am having a really good time. Totally in awe I am watching the flocks of puffins that pass us by, and I am hypnotised by the seagulls that race up to our stern and then continue gliding in the lee of our sail. They are looking me straight in the eyes and get so close that I can almost touch them.

North Cape & Hammerfest

16th July, 2000

In the distance we can see the North Cape surrounded by a fog bank. One minute it is visible and next it is not. It is not quite true that North Cape is the most northern part of Europe. A little beyond North Cape is Knivskjelodden, which reaches just a little bit more to the north. But since there are no roads to Knivskjelodden all the tourists flock to the North Cape plateau on the island of Magerøya, which is connected to the Norwegian mainland by tunnel. I wonder if the daily flock of tourists can see anything, let alone us. The sky looks weird and I am staying about a mile and a half to starboard of our course as we are off a lee shore. The seagulls that surround *Fereale* have either white wings, black wings, speckled wings, or grey wings. Suddenly I hear a splash and then another and another and see dolphins dancing, leaping, jumping and playing around *Fereale*. Gordon was really disappointed that I had not called him. It was important for me, though, that he was sleeping, as we have been able to give each other four hours or more and feel very rested because of it.

We rounded the North Cape just as I was cosy and snug in my bunk. Begrudgingly I got up and dressed in the warmest clothes I could find. Even though there is not much to see on the horizon it is still a special moment, one we celebrated with shrimps and champagne. Then it was back to bed for me for another couple of hours of sleep.

It is difficult to find time to write as we are either concentrating hard on navigation, hand steering, resting, or I am preparing food. Real tiredness is striking us both and we are looking forward to our arrival in Hammerfest in

North Cape

some four or five hours' time. It takes guts to sail here, even if I say so myself, as everything is so big, powerful and impressive. One can see at first hand here how the earth was created. No country we have ever seen can compare with what Norway has to offer. We did not arrive in Hammerfest, the world's most northern town, until 10pm and moored up alongside a fishing boat.

17th July, 2000
Spirit of Aeolus and *Nomad* still managed to arrive ahead of us and both are moored up closer to the town centre. Our spot is not a bad one and seems to be away from the probing eyes of the tourists. Being in a fishing harbour I soon found a laundrette and took to hoisting my bike up the steep vertical ladder to the quayside, leaving Gordon to his chores. Before long I met up with Elsbeth, reunited with *Spirit* now and with an ulcerated leg that was well on the mend.

18th July, 2000
We have not seen darkness now for a month or more. From a distance we watched *Nomad* leave and expect that *Spirit of Aeolus* will follow suit. For the first time in months we are taking things easy; taking time to have a haircut, cycle through the town together and prepare *Fereale* for the next leg. We are

Magic of the Arctic

Typical fjord

also enjoying being on our own; the three boats just meeting up once or twice a week. André, with *Endring*, is in his home country now and will be doing his own thing from now on. He is based in Stavanger where his job is waiting for him. Ray Glaister will be laying up his boat, *Babaji*, in Narvik for the winter. Next year he intends to take his time to explore the area around there. What a nice thing to do if you don't have to work anymore and are retired.

19th July, 2000

It is 6am and we are on our way once more, both of us having had a good night's sleep. Hammerfest has proved to be a lovely stopover. We are really going to enjoy our next four weeks, as we don't feel so much on the edge of the world as we did when sailing along the Kola Peninsula. Here we have been able to get back onto an even keel. The harbour masters, when we can find them, are pleased to see us and can't do enough to help. The scenery is spectacular. With everything so big here it takes twice as long to cross a fjord as one thinks it should. Every time I think we have nearly arrived at our landmark we still have miles to go. You come to appreciate the scale of a mountain when there is a ship next to it, looking just like a dinky toy.

The start of the day was rainy, then overcast with the humidity rising all the time. The wind has picked up and we are sailing nicely now in the company of lots of puffins—a delightful sight. They are such comical birds, with their quick flapping wings and funny red beaks. Gordon is resting and looks very comfortable. Me, I am letting the autopilot do all the work and spend my time writing and keeping an eye on our course. It is 5pm and in an hour and a half we should arrive at Skjervøya, an island with a little hidden harbour, difficult to identify from a distance. All I can see is a big, dark blob of a rock amongst the snow-clad mountains. The landscape is amazing and the peace it brings is even greater. Our cockpit GPS is having great problems and we have to go down below to check our ground course on the other set. Still, we have managed so far, even when they both failed to work for a while.

With great difficulty we moored up along a quayside not meant for the likes of us, but with permission granted we stayed the night. Gordon received an email from someone at his office, which unfortunately made him think of work again. To be back in touch with the girls and the rest of our family is great though, and we look forward to opening our mailbox in the evenings.

Tromsø

20th July, 2000

We tend to leave early every morning—the best time of day for us. With the sky already blue and pink in colour, it is an honour to sail here; to discover new places, each one more beautiful than the other. The wind is all over the place. One minute we need to wear full oilskins and the next just a light top. When we left Skjervøya we saw small dolphins, but were never close enough to photograph them. The puffins are also too quick for me and tend to dive under the water just as I am ready with my camera. We are taking the recommended inland route from Hammerfest to Tromsø called the Indreleia. Like this we can take inland routes almost all the way to Bergen. We should arrive in Tromsø, a university town and one of Norway's biggest fishing harbours, at about seven tonight.

It is 2pm and suddenly the weather has turned for the worse, something we saw coming. With the wind dead on the nose *Fereale* powers her way through the waves into the Tromsø sunset. We have hit the blackest sky we have ever seen, with zero visibility, and let ourselves be guided by our radar and GPS. The waves are decorated with white crests, but *Fereale* is strong and her engine keeps on going even when our speed drops to zero from time to time. Finally we arrive in Tromsø to the delight of *Nomad* and *Spirit of Aeolus*, who were aware of the bad weather and had wondered about our safety. There was lots of activity on *Spirit* as Willem had discovered the reason for the strange noises that had been coming from their engine room. Every one of the four bolts that had been holding their engine in place had finally snapped in half! He was lucky

135

to have found a local sailor with golden hands to help him, someone with the knowledge and skill to lift up their engine and put it back in place. It would have been unthinkable if the last of the bolts had snapped whilst still in Russia.

Priority number one was to call our children, after which we relaxed on board *Nomad* following a dinner invitation. We never have a problem doing this with Brenda and Alan.

21st July, 2000

It is quite funny; I have no idea what day of the week it is. We are too busy partying, fixing things or being on the move. Gordon's day started with helping Alan get the air out of his fuel filters. *Spirit*'s problems have in the meantime been solved and by lunchtime she had slipped her moorings and was gone. The destination of *Fereale*, *Nomad* and *Endring* is Andenes, some eighty miles from here. André has decided to take things easy from now on and will take a week to get there.

22nd July, 2000

It is early in the morning and people are setting up their stalls on the market. They mainly sell things for the tourists like Norwegian jumpers, reindeer skins, woodcarvings, fish and shrimps. Feeling a little like explorers we decided to visit the Polar Museum. There is a replica of an emergency camp set up by the Dutchman Willem Barentsz on Novaya Zemlya back in 1596. Not having good charts, he did not really know where he was and made the mistake of passing north of the island and got stuck in the ice. By using the wood from their ship, he and his crew made a camp, hoping to survive the savage winter. Barentsz himself died, but a few of his crew lived to tell the tale and managed to return to Holland. It was not until 1871 that the remains of the camp were discovered. All of this became a lot more interesting for me after I had found Novaya Zemlya on the world map and noticed that it was only a few days' sail from the Kola Peninsula where we had recently sailed. We also learned about the many expeditions Amundsen undertook. He was the first man to sail through the Northwest Passage to Alaska, in 1906. Gordon and I saw his sailing vessel, the *Gjøa*, in the National Maritime Museum in Oslo when we lived there in 1980. We also visited his ship, the *Fram*, which took him to the South Pole in 1910. His main interest was in making magnetic observations. Then there was the voyage of Nansen, who had a theory that if he allowed his ship to get stuck in the ice it would drift all the way to the North Pole and across the Arctic Ocean. His ship left Vardø and headed for Siberia where she got firmly stuck. Nansen soon realised, however, that she was not going to drift to the North Pole after all and that he would have to continue his journey on foot. Together with one of his crew and with dogs, sledges and canoes they set off. Food was in short supply and sadly they had to shoot their dogs. Eventually they reached some land, rocks or caves, where they built a hut and survived on seals and polar bears. In springtime they continued their journey south and were eventually picked up by a British expedition ship and taken back to Vardø. They weighed more than at the beginning of their journey thanks to the protein-rich food they had enjoyed. The crew who were left behind on his ship, and who thought Nansen had perished, also managed to get back. The displays in the museum showed us how they shot the polar bears and what was used for trapping arctic foxes and seals. Not only that, but we could see the clothes that they wore and how they made them out of fur, the skiing equipment that they used, and how they maintained their tools.

In glorious sunshine *Nomad* and *Fereale* tanked up with diesel and set off, leaving Tromsø behind.

It is 3pm and we are passing through a narrow stretch called Ryøyastrammen, to the North of the island of Ryøya . A huge amount of water has to go through this passage. *Fereale*, being strong, is coping well, even with the water boiling and whirling around us. With about five knots of tide against us progress is very slow. *Nomad*, being a lighter boat, is well ahead. The scenery is magnificent, with a large bird colony to port of us. It is quite alpine here, but the alpine meadows are at sea level. All that is missing are the cows with bells around their necks. To see all of this from our boat is quite strange, and it is hard to believe that we are in the Arctic Circle.

At eight in the evening we arrived in Botnhamn, a lovely harbour town at the entrance to the sea, and moor up alongside a fishing boat. Brenda and Alan, who arrived ahead of us, are on the other side of the harbour. Our holiday really started when we arrived in Norway, as what we are experiencing now is why we go cruising. We wonder if anyone is alive out here, as we can see about twenty houses but it is completely silent. We still have a schedule to keep but this is far less frantic than pushing our way through Russia. Back to reality and the question of when to leave tomorrow, as we need to be on the right side of a ferocious tide to take us through a narrow sound. The decision was made to leave at five in the morning.

Andenes

23rd July, 2000

We can always count on Brenda and Alan, who are never late and always stick to their schedule. Coming from the Channel Islands, they know better than anyone what it is to sail in such waters. This tide is one we can't afford to miss, as the gap between the two islands is narrow and the current fierce. The surroundings are littered with half submerged rocks (mountain tops), and our eyes are glued to the navigation. In half an hour we shall turn the corner and will be able to hoist our main. One should definitely not be here in bad weather or in the dark, or fog!

No more engine noise at last as once through the gap *Fereale* lifted her skirts towards the island of Andøya, still further north than Murmansk. We are making a detour to Vesterålen, a group of islands north of the famous Lofoten. We have heard that they arrange whaling safaris from the capital of Andenes, in the northern part of the archipelago. Here the edge of the continental shelf is closer to land than anywhere else along the Norwegian coast. This is where the sperm whales feed, a voyage of about an hour out to sea and where the depth suddenly changes from two hundred and fifty metres to two thousand—a place to be avoided in bad weather. We have decided to go on one of these trips, together with Brenda and Alan, rather than using our own boats. The weather is worsening all the time and it seems a good idea.

Alan and Brenda were there to take our lines, such a nice welcome as we are always pleased to see each other safely back in harbour. We were all tired and in need of a good night's sleep, but not before a little get together first.

The harbour at Andenes

24th July, 2000

We slept well and met up with Brenda and Alan on the way to the whaling museum. Like us they were wearing oilskins and had cameras and binoculars at the ready. At the museum scientists and students from many different countries do research on the behaviour of the various species of whales seen off Andøya. Such studies include acoustics, social behaviour, mating, the age of the whales, photo identification and many more topics. Our guide was one of these students who later joined us on the vessel *M/S Reine*. But first we watched a video, which showed us the different species of whales that can be seen here all the year round; the minke whale, the killer whale, the fin whale and the pilot whale. Finally it was time to be told about the sperm whale, the one we were most likely to see. With my notepad forever at the ready I could not write fast enough. It seems that the bull can grow as large as eighteen metres or more and can weigh fifty tonnes. They use their white palates and teeth as a lure, teeth that can weigh up to a kilo each. The size of the whales that feed here at the moment tells the scientists that almost all are sexually mature males. Females do not travel the big oceans, it seems. Most of the sperm whales, when they dive to hunt in the deep canyon off Andøya, feed within a range of two to six hundred metres of depth. This is where there is what they call a scattering layer of food like cod, squid and blue whiting. But they can dive much deeper than that—up to a few thousand meters—in search of giant squid. A sperm whale eats up to a tonne of squid a day and the bigger the better. They dive all the way to the seabed, weighing themselves down with their huge heads, to find the biggest of them all. But at a depth of a thousand metres the pressure of the water is too much for their lungs, causing them to collapse. Only the vast store of oxygen in their muscles and blood enables them to continue swimming. After some thirteen minutes their bodies will have shrunk to half their size. No other mammal in the world can dive deeper or for longer than the sperm whale, which is able to hold its breath for two hours or more.

They navigate by way of echolocation, a high-pitched clicking sound. A sound they listen to when it is reflected back, having stunned their prey from an incredible range. Sperm whale clicks are the loudest measured sound created by any animal. Another way they stun the pray is by creating shock waves with their tails. The giant squid, some twenty metres long, is not easily stunned and does not like to be eaten! He will fight with his tentacles to resist capture, and squirts out clouds of ink as a smoke screen in the hope of escape. Many sperm whales have strange looking circular scars on their heads; scars made by the tentacles of the giant squid during their fight for life.

When they come up to breathe their first breath is very loud and sounds just like an explosion, which can be heard from a great distance. Desperate for air they head for the surface like torpedoes and literally shoot out of the water, after which they fall back in with a tremendous splash. There they rest for a while, taking a few deep breaths to recover, before diving to the depths once more. This is the time when we are able to observe them, when they are resting, breathing and spouting oil and water some two metres into the air.

Together with other tourists we boarded the *M/S Reine*, having been given seasick tablets in preparation for our rather rough voyage. We found a good spot on deck and wedged ourselves in. With delight I watched the enthusiastic marine biology students who were our guides. They told us that every trip out on the *M/S Reine* is as special as their first. Occasionally they looked up at the pilothouse as our captain, a reformed whale hunter, was most likely to spot them first. The four of us, having got our sea legs by now, watched everyone around us being miserably sick. Then the moment came to call: "There she blows," some fifteen miles out at sea and at a depth of nine hundred metres. We had

Sperm whale off Andenes

been warned to protect our cameras from the waves that occasionally came over the railings, but nevertheless were fully christened when trying to take our first picture. Not one but several whales wallowed in the water, in a slow and graceful way. Resting and breathing and so gentle

Brenda, Alan and me on whale watch

looking, then diving down again in a long curve showing their huge distinctive tails last of all. They did not seem disturbed by the presence of the *M/S Reine*, who tried to keep a distance of some fifty metres so as not to stress the animals. All together we saw five sperm whales, but our captain had seen many more. Brenda and Alan, not content with just watching the mammals, had dinner out in the evening and tasted them too.

Time once again to prepare *Fereale* for departure in the hope that the strong winds will have blown themselves out during the night.

25th July, 2000

Luck was with us and after a slow start we left the difficult harbour of Andenes, littered with rocks and vardes, pointing in all directions. Vardes are stone towers painted black, often with a white stripe. Typically on top there is an arm pointing in the safe direction. A little bit like traffic policemen. We watched *Nomad* leave ahead of us and for a moment I looked on in horror as I realised I had given them confusing directions, given to me by a fisherman. But, as always, they knew very well what they were doing and were just fine.

In spite of the sun shining it is arctic cold and both of us are wearing woollies, balaclavas, hats and gloves. In a huge swell we hoisted our sails and watched *Nomad* disappear in the distance. It is beautiful yet very strange sailing in between all this granite.

At last some competition and we pull in the sheets as a fast square-rigger astern of us is threatening to catch up. It is the first boat that we have seen today apart from *Nomad*. With a speed of seven knots we sailed into Harstad on the island of Hinnøya at seven in the evening. Brenda and Alan, on another pontoon, were well into relaxation mode having found the Vinmonopolet still open. Did my eyes deceive me, or did I see John Knap loading his bags on board *Nomad*? John was *Babaji*'s crew who we thought had flown back to England. The truth was that he was making a slow passage south, taking local ferries and buses. Meeting up quite by chance, Brenda and Alan had offered him sanctuary for the night. Whilst they dined out we socialised with a Polish boat on the same pontoon as us who was on its way to Spitsbergen. A funny looking boat, with a huge polar bear painted on her bow. Her captain, who fitted the part, wore polar underwear wherever he went and had a white beard. Amazed, I watched not one but six crew members appear from its tiny hull. A hull made out of 3 mm plating, which seemed thin to us when one is heading for the ice. Whilst he praised us that we were able to handle *Fereale* with just the two of us, we in turn praised him for coping with so many. A far more difficult task I would think. Then I realised that they were probably paying crew.

26th July, 2000

Every day we look forward to the next and are ready to explore more of Norway's beautiful coastline. Early in the morning we quietly slipped our mooring lines, leaving Alan and Brenda to sleep off their sore heads. The further south we get the more likely it is that we will come across more sailing boats. We shall have to get used to the crowded harbours again in two months' time when we are back in Holland! *Fereale* has acquired a few rusty spots here and there during our trip, but the rest of her complexion is glowing. We have got used to the idea of taking our home with us wherever we go, but I admit that it was strange at first. Of course, we carry the same responsibility whether she is our home or not.

We are motor sailing to arrive at the Tjeldsund, a narrow sound, in time to catch the tide. It is always an incredible experience for us as well as *Fereale* to cope with the strong currents, which should not be attempted on spring tides or in bad weather. Our stop for the night was Lødingen, where we arrived at a decent time of day and were able to return Brenda and Alan's hospitality. Being content with whatever the cook was able to produce, we had a good time on board *Fereale* and discussed our next leg to Bodø. Most evenings we receive emails from our family. Knowing what is going on back home, and vice versa, completes our happiness.

27th July, 2000
Slowly we glided past rows of islands, just peaks of mountains that stick out above the water. Our spinnaker carried us past the dramatic scenery of the Lofoten, of which, unfortunately, we saw very little. With great excitement we spotted the triangular dorsal fins of six killer whales, at a distance of some three miles. The fin of a bull can reach a height of 1.8 metres and is easy to spot. One after another they jumped vertically out of the water showing off their white bellies and creating huge fountains. We were glued to the scene and only occasionally looked at where we were going. They hunt in packs, large or small, just like wolves. Some eat fish, others seals, dolphins or even whales. The Norwegian killer whales usually feed close to the surface, in the upper twenty metres where they find small schools of herring. Unlike the sperm whale, they are only down for a short time.

Just after Gordon had gone down for a nap I witnessed something strange on the horizon. Like a mirage, rocks were appearing out of nowhere. After plotting our position three times in twenty minutes and still not finding rocks anywhere on the chart I became rather worried. Totally confused by this I woke Gordon, and together we decided that this was the strangest phenomenon we had ever come across. It *was* a mirage, created by the clouds together with the intense heat of the sun.

There is not enough wind to sail so we are motoring. Gordon is taking advantage of the boat not being at an angle for a change and is draining water out of the bottom of our day tank. Our main diesel tanks are situated in both keels of the boat and there is still water in one of them, which we have not managed to get out. The only way he can drain it off is after he has transferred it to our day tank. It has to be checked several times a day if it is not too rough outside and the water has had an opportunity settle. *Fereale*, grateful for all the attention she is getting, rewards us by bringing us safely from landfall to landfall. Feeling a little jealous I have to make do with looking after myself. It is nine o'clock in the evening and we are approaching the town of Bodø, framed by tall snow-capped mountains. It has been a hot day and we might

In my element

just as well be somewhere in the Mediterranean. To our surprise we manage to find a place astern of *Nomad* in the very busy harbour, mainly occupied by powerboats. The Norwegians don't sail much on the west coast of Norway, as the wind is either fierce, fluky, or non-existent. The sailing boats we do see are usually foreign.

28th July, 2000

Taking advantage of the wonderful sunshine Brenda and I did our hand-washing and the two boats are looking most decorative. No cooking for me tonight as we have been invited to celebrate Alan's 60th birthday on board *Nomad*. Instead we cycled around the town and did not waste any time on mundane things like food shopping. Our plan is to sail towards glacier country tomorrow, and Gordon has left to get some charts. At last I had some time to myself and relaxed in the cockpit with my concertina, something I do when I feel happy and content. My playing was heard by a young live-aboard on the same pontoon as us. He joined me and said that he was a professional musician, that he played the clarinet, and was currently playing at a music festival in Bodø. Instantly I stopped playing and felt most embarrassed. Not only was *he* a professional musician, but so was the man on the boat next to him who played the violin and was apparently one of Norway's best. This man lived on his boat, together with his wife and two young children. We had a lovely chat and watched the little ones catch fish after fish from the edge of our pontoon, a daily event apparently, as their cat needed feeding. At 6 o'clock in the evening, both Gordon and I, looking our very best, boarded *Nomad* carrying a bottle of champagne. We enjoyed a fantastic three-course dinner cooked by Brenda. None of us could have wished for a nicer evening as my clarinet friend joined our party and serenaded Alan. We improvised and even played together for a while which was a great honour for a novice like me.

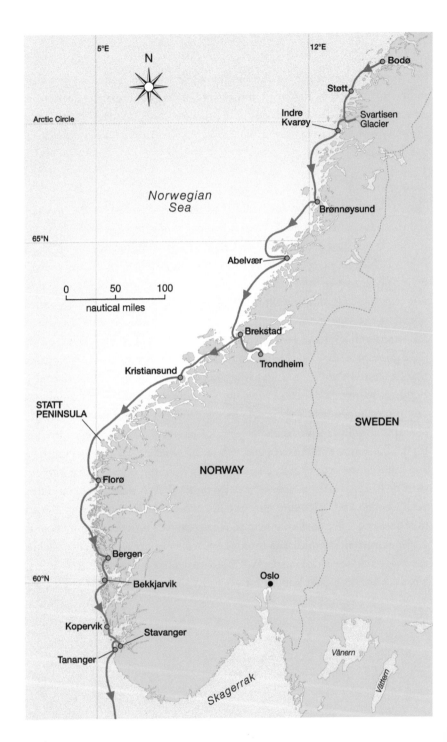

Bodø to Stavanger

Learning the Art of Fishing

29th July, 2000

The sun has not stopped shining and we are on our way. We don't know Brenda and Alan's plans, other than that we shall meet them in Trondheim in a few days' time. Our day has turned out somewhat differently than planned, as our quick stop at Støtt to tank-up with diesel has turned into an overnight stay.

Carefully we zigzagged in-between the rocks and soon found our slot on the only pontoon available. Whilst Gordon disappeared in search of the harbour master, I watched a little fishing boat coming in, occupied by a man and wife team. Their buckets were overflowing with fish and I watched from a distance how they cleaned their catch, making a mental note of what fishing gear and tools they used. When Gordon came back we introduced ourselves and found out that they were a local couple called Kurt and Brigit. My Norwegian was truly put to the test at this point, as they did not speak any English. Kurt was amused to see my enthusiasm and offered to fill our tiny freezer. Before long the four of us were drinking tea in our saloon, after which Kurt offered to take us out on his boat and teach me the art of fishing.

Brigit, although obliging, was hungry and wanted to eat something first. Next we all got into their car and were driven to their home, which overlooked the sea and harbour, and enjoyed a delicious Norwegian tea, with homemade bread and cloudberry jam. "Here people trust each other," he said, "and you don't need to lock up your boat, house or car." Not only were they interested in sharing their culture with us, they were also curious about ours. Something we were happy to share. It was quite tiring, as everything I said or learned had

Brigit and Kurt

to be translated back to Gordon.

Not long after, we sped off in his little boat, with Brigit looking as white as a sheet at the back of the tiny cabin, suffering from seasickness. Kurt knew every rock in sight and ventured where *Fereale* would never be able to go. "This is sea eagle country," he said, pointing out several, either flying or sitting on rocks protecting their territories. With a wingspan of some two and a half metres they were an amazing sight. Both Gordon and I were in our element and totally stunned by the beauty of it all.

Suddenly we stopped, as the fish finder had located a shoal. Under instruction I let out a hundred and fifty metres of fishing line, put the brake on and started pulling, to the great amusement of the others. Although the line felt very heavy, I was determined not to show this and pretended to be strong. I thought it was the lead at the end of the line that had made it heavy and was quietly thinking that they should have invented a machine for this. The pretence that the line was light had worked and Kurt thought our efforts had been in vain. "Bring in the line, please," he said "and we'll have another go elsewhere." But, to our utter surprise, I had caught five kilos of fish in less than ten minutes!

Brigit, aware that I would not know what to do, grabbed one three-kilo cod through its eyes with her bare fingers, took the hook out and dropped him in the bucket. Was this what I was expected to do? Was this my dream? I shuddered and so did Gordon. But I had shown all this enthusiasm for the sport after all, and could not very well pull away from it now. Hopefully the next time we would be fishing from the decks of *Fereale* and would need to manage by ourselves one way or another. With that in mind, and with a scrunched-up face, I took the next two fish off the line in the same way as Brigit had done. Now it was Gordon's turn and we sped off to another location. He was equally determined, but to no

My first catch

avail. With disappointment in his face he handed the line over to me and looked totally baffled as I hauled in another three kilos. It was time to go home, as both our freezers were full. Once back in harbour we said goodbye to Kurt and Brigit, having taught us yet another aspect of life at sea.

30th July, 2000

Today we shall be crossing south of the Arctic Circle and will be heading towards glacier country. Although we have seen a few glaciers in the Alps, we have never sailed amongst them. It is arctic cold and we are wearing the full gear, once again taking the beautiful inland route towards Nordfjord. There we will make a four-hour detour to see the glaciers. Once again the wind is dead on the nose and we can't raise our sails. The mountains around us are covered in grey clouds but *Fereale* pushes on unrelentingly. We have to be in Trondheim by Friday, which is our rendezvous day with *Nomad* and perhaps *Spirit*. To be there in time we need to average a distance of sixty miles a day. If we are over two days late Alan will alert the coastguard. Our barometer shows a shining sun and we hope it comes before we reach the great monster fjord.

Gordon was first to spot a group of killer whales in the distance. They were jumping high out of the water, which was a welcome distraction. We are just passing a globe stuck on a rock, marking the point where we cross south of the Arctic Circle. The scenic section of the Nordfjord is lying dead ahead of us. Unfortunately the mountains are still covered in fog and it has started to rain. The waterfalls that come down the sheer cliffs either side of us are awe-inspiring and tumble down like strands of wavy hair into the crystal clear water. Rocks that look as if they are ready to roll down on top of us are hanging as if by a thread from the steep mountainsides. We have acquired a passenger, a tired little bird in need of a rest. If only we had some sun and a blue sky.

The wind is circulating around the mountains, coming from all directions. Totally awestruck we slowly motored towards the end of the fjord. It is here that the large Svartisen glacier, one of Norway's most spectacular, almost tumbles to the sea where it changes the colour of the water to an almost unreal bluey green.

Below the Svartisen glacier

We are only experiencing half of the grandeur of this place, as we are unable to see the tops of the mountains covered by clouds. It is quite something to get here with *Fereale* and we feel like taking some snow back with us as a souvenir. But anchoring is not a good idea in these fluky winds. Being at the foot of a glacier and still at sea level is unique and the atmosphere special. Sadly we turned *Fereale* around and headed towards the delightful island of Indre Kvarøy where we did not arrive until 9pm.

31st July, 2000
When we left a force four from the north was forecast. We were excited at the prospect of sailing again, even though it was not long before the fog and rain descended on us once more. It was a relaxing kind of day nevertheless with Gordon already planning tomorrow's route. The scenery around us is as lovely as ever. Occasionally we see a sailing boat, still very rare and mostly foreign. Also the further south we get the darker it is getting, which feels very strange. We had an email from Willem and Elsbeth last night, which informed us that they were only a short distance ahead of us. They were at anchor and had climbed the Torghatten mountain, which has a big circular hole in it. They had needed a tow from a fellow sailor a few days ago owing to a defective starter motor. Willem said that he had given away the bottle of whisky that Gordon had given him in Russia, as a thank you for a tow that they had given us. Let's hope that this kind man does not need to give it away again for the same purpose!

1st August, 2000
After a long day we arrived at Brønnøysund, where we managed to replenish our food stock just before the shops closed. We have a lot to do, before we can turn in for the night, the boat needs cleaning, the water wants topping up, the diesel and oil need transferring and the cooling water needs to be checked. Only then can we start thinking of planning tomorrow's safe route, with waypoints and positions.

2nd August, 2000
It is 7am and we are on our way to catch a strong tide that is to take us through a narrow sound. The clouds are much higher now and give us a better view

of the mountains. Even though it is beautiful taking the inland route, it is very tiring and we have decided to do it differently from now on. We shall go around the outside instead, with fewer waypoints enabling us to get more rest.

Strong winds accompanied us all day and we were tired and pleased to arrive in Abelvær. It took three attempts before we managed to tie up alongside a quay, covered with barnacle-entrusted tyres. With such a strong wind we did not fancy anchoring, which would have been our only other option. This is no place for sailing boats, but that is half of the attraction after all. At last we were able to relax, but not until we had spoken to some curious locals, who said we could stay for one night. We discovered that we had arrived at a salmon processing farm and watched with fascination as a big ship came in, low on her waterline. She was filled with salmon that had been collected from farms in the surrounding areas. After she moored up, the next hour or so was used to pump out the many tons of salmon contained in her bilges. She heeled dangerously at times, and then the captain of the ship compensated the balance by pumping in more water. But no more time for niceties as tomorrow will be bringing yet another early start.

3rd August, 2000
On our way and *Fereale* is carrying full sail.

It did not take long before we were out at sea, where the wind took hold and pushed *Fereale* along. Looking astern we noticed that *Nomad* was following us, and was going as fast as a rocket. But it was not long before the wind proved too strong for their liking and they disappeared between the mountains. Both Gordon and I have been able to catch up on some sleep at last. It is very nice not to hear the sound of the engine for a change, and once more be out in the open sea. With a few sail changes on the way we are literally flying. In the evening we heard a call over the VHF: "Russian vessel, Russian vessel." Looking around and seeing no Russian vessel in sight, we wondered if somebody was calling us, perhaps. The Russian and Dutch flags look similar; instead of our red, white and blue, the Russian flag shows white, blue and red.

It is the first time since St Petersburg that we have seen lights on the shore, in other words, there is now less daylight. Once in Trondheim we found *Spirit of Aeolus* safely tucked away, her crew fast asleep, like the rest of the town. An example we soon followed.

Trondheim

It was in Trondheim that *Spirit*'s crew left as planned, from now on it would be just Willem and Elsbeth. I was pleased for them, but got the impression that they much preferred having crew. Soon they sailed away, leaving us to a normal kind of day with lots of jobs to be done. The day was pleasantly interrupted by a visit from a couple belonging to the local sailing club. Their names were Ola and Gunn Bergslien, serious sailors, who had crossed the Atlantic and sailed in the Caribbean and Azores. They told us that they are always intrigued when a foreign boat comes into their harbour, and that they had stopped to see if there was anything they could do for us. They were most interested in our voyage through Russia and picked our brains for any information they could get. Ola, who is a doctor at the local hospital, also works for the local Search and Rescue team (SAR). He goes out in helicopters in the most atrocious weather and rescues people from the sea. Gunn works at the same hospital as Ola, and together they make a great team. Ola has an incredibly technical mind and was keen to help Gordon with any problems he might have had of that nature. Somehow there was an immediate trust between the two men, and it did not take long before they were fixing one of our long overdue projects. Our radar, for instance, which had been showing a deviation of some ten degrees ever since we had owned it. A problem Gordon had not got round to fixing yet. Ola knew about these things, dived into it and together they got it to within one degree of deviation. He was intrigued to see that our boat was equipped with a GMDSS radio, as his boat was the first to be equipped with it in Norway.

155

It is still very new here, but also in Holland. He decided to test our ability to work with it, saying that it was important for us, as well as the coastal stations, to get into the practice of how to handle calls. He suggested that we gave the local coastal station a call, give them our MMSI number and ask them to call us back. This we did and saw that our call had been received, but we also noticed that our VHF had not acknowledged their return call to us. After fiddling with some wires we tried again and this time the coastal station succeeded in reaching us. They said that they had been delighted to help us, as they were eager to get in some practice, too.

Brenda and Alan, having arrived later in afternoon, were also included in a dinner invitation at their flat that evening, Gunn insisting that I brought along my washing. It is wonderful when one meets such genuine people, total strangers whose kindness can leave such a lasting impression. What helped of course was that they were fellow sailors and understood our needs.

Our plan to leave the following day turned out rather differently than expected.

6th August, 2000

All night long the wind howled in our rigging. Nevertheless, come morning, *Nomad* set sail and left. We had not yet switched on our VHF so were unaware that they had tried to contact us. They had hoped to tell us that they were on their way back and thus save us the bother of casting off. Soaking wet, they returned back to the harbour, meeting us on our way out. Although less wet, we experienced the same and also returned for yet another day in harbour. Before long Ola and Gunn paid us another visit. The rest of the day was spent going over charts and technical items, and Ola treating my infected eye. Brenda and Alan wisely turned down the offer to go to the cinema that night to watch *The Perfect Storm*. It had an unsettling effect on both Gordon and me and neither of us slept a wink that night. The noise in the rigging did not help matters, of course.

7th August, 2000

Today we have no alternative but to leave. Brenda and Alan are having a hard time and we watch *Nomad* slamming into every wave. *Fereale* has a more comfortable motion, which is due to her much heavier and fuller hull.

Both of us are taking the inland route just to be on the safe side, but still the weather is unpredictable, with slight visibility one minute, and zero visibility the next. Our radar no longer has any deviation and we are wondering how we ever managed without it before. In the pouring rain we arrived in Brekstad, a nice little harbour, with Brenda and Alan there to take our lines. Again an unplanned meeting, as we never know where any of us might end up. Having arrived a few hours ahead of us, they offered us a warm meal and a stiff drink, after which we raised our glasses and bless our wonderful lives.

8th August, 2000
Once again gale force winds dead on the nose. We soon discovered that we were not making any headway and both *Nomad* and *Fereale* returned to harbour, having had their christening for the day. Instead, the heating went on and I was able to relax for a change, but not so for Gordon. Our optimistic hope has always been that by October he would be working again somewhere around the globe. The closer we get to home base, however, the more worried he is getting about our future. A positive start had to be made by looking up all the email addresses of the various agents, together with composing letters with résumés attached.

9th August, 2000
At 5am we looked outside and decided to wait till six, and at six we decided to wait till seven. It is raining cats and dogs and the wind is howling around us. Slowly we are preparing *Fereale* for our inevitable departure towards Kristiansund. Brenda and Alan, who left some time ago, have already given us updates on the conditions in the fjord. Their routine is to have breakfast on the way, unlike us. I keep thinking about fishing and would dearly like to stock up my freezer. The little fishing boats around us all seem to be using the same reels that Kurt and Brigit used on their boat. Gordon has at last decided to allow me to raid the bank when time allows. After all, he will also benefit from the experience.

There seems to be something wrong with our electric autopilot and we think that the compass attached to our mast needs more alcohol in its brain. A nuisance, as from now on we shall have to steer by hand. The conditions at sea are choppy and I have positioned myself on two fender boards behind our steering column. The barometer has been rising by one millibar every hour and things are looking up at last. Life is good on board, and *Fereale* has proved time and again to be the perfect boat for us.

It is 3pm and the sun is shining. I have just been reading up about Kristiansund in a Norwegian pilot book, trying to find out about the visitors' harbour. The town is connected to the mainland via bridges and underwater tunnels. We are really looking forward to visiting this city as everyone who has been there has recommended it.

It was not until 6pm that our compass on the mast behaved to some extent, and the fjord had returned once more to a reasonably normal state. Both of us have had plenty of rest and feel that we could go on like this forever. The dusk has coloured the mountains in shades of blue and grey, the ones in the foreground darker, then lighter and lighter, all the while the clouds are showing their silver lining. A really beautiful sight.

Kristiansund

Kristiansund

10th August, 2000

The day was spent pottering about in harbour, and in brilliant sunshine we cycled into town. The houses surrounding the harbour are painted in a multitude of colours. All of them have pitched roofs and are built in the shelter of the low mountains. The highlight of our day was, of course, the purchase of our famous fishing reel; some much-needed local charts and shrimps for lunch. We have noticed how expensive the shrimps are getting, the further south we get. With the problem of our compass still on our minds Gordon decided to climb the mast. This is where he discovered that sticky bearings were the real reason why our compass was not working properly. The bearings move OK when the boat is rolling, but stick when the boat is pitching. Thinking it was a reasonably easy problem to solve he set to work. The twenty-one-year-old nylon bolts that were the culprit did not budge however and not having the time or the tools to do the job properly he had to admit defeat. For the last time our bikes came out to cycle to another part of the harbour, where we watched old boats being restored using the old traditional methods.

It is now 8pm and time to access our email and have a serious look at the charts. Tomorrow we will be heading towards Bergen, some two hundred and sixty nautical miles from here, with a possible stop on the way. We shall have to round a nasty corner called Statt, a point on the Norwegian chart that has a bad reputation. It will take possibly two nights to get to Bergen, depending on the wind strength and direction. Brenda and Alan have been talking about it for days.

11th August, 2000

It will be a shame to leave Kristiansund but in spite of that we are eager to sail again. Not in a hurry to leave we took our time to get organised, and dutifully informed the coastguard of our intentions. A friendly voice on the other side wished us a good journey and confirmed the good weather conditions for rounding Statt. One must not get it wrong as the sea can be dangerous there, owing to the varying depths, especially in a strong north-westerly wind and with an ebb tide. It is Friday and, if we can maintain our current speed of six knots, we will arrive in Bergen by Sunday. There we hope to have a jolly good knees-up, as the three remaining boats from the northern fleet will part company. There is a huge swell and *Fereale* is rolling into the first of two nights at sea. If we did not have to alter course our next landfall would be Scotland.

12th August, 2000

It is early in the morning and with a force four behind us we have nearly rounded Statt. The seas are big, and I can only imagine having to worry about this bulge of a corner in bad weather. I am feeling very pleased with myself having hoisted the staysail whilst Gordon slept. A simple job like that demands a lot of care when alone on watch as Gordon, once in dreamland, would never hear me should I fall in. We have promised each other to be good and always clip on and wear lifejackets. But soon the sail had to come down again, as the wind changed direction and turned the sea into confusion. Having to work just a little bit too hard for our living, we decided to head for the shore. My neck, shoulders, arms and legs are feeling the brunt of the intense steering by hand in the heavy swell. Gordon, whose main job it had been to concentrate on the chart work, navigated us safely into Florø.

13th August, 2000

In the early morning hours we quietly slipped our mooring lines and navigated *Fereale* in and around the lit buoys and lighthouses back to the open sea. Whereas Gordon has always found navigating by night easier than by day, I am only slowly starting to enjoy this. Another tiring day, as the wind once more increased in strength and howled around us together with the fog descending, bringing the visibility down to zero. We are in yet another area marked on the chart with 'Dangerous waves'. The sea is totally confused and all over the place, but in the shelter of our cockpit we are dry and feel neither wind nor water.

To enter Bergen at night is an impressive sight, with the lights of the town built on a mountain slope, together with the many illuminated suspension bridges. We moored up at a picturesque old waterfront, astern of *Nomad* and *Spirit of Aeolus*. Whilst securing our mooring lines Gordon, to his horror, came face to face with a huge rat on the quayside. Knowing very well the damage they can do to the intestines of a boat, we quickly locked our vents and hatches. We did not dare to disturb Willem or Alan, who were still fast asleep and unaware of the nasty predators.

14th August, 2000

In the morning the others discovered, to their surprise, that we had arrived in the middle of the night. For the next three days, we partied and socialised, the skippers and crew being chuffed at their achievement. We celebrated Elsbeth's birthday and decided that the boats should meet up once more but this time in Stavanger for Brenda's birthday later in the month.

17th August, 2000

Although *Nomad* and *Spirit of Aeolus* left Bergen after lunch, *Fereale* stayed behind. Being on our own we finally had time to concentrate once more on solving some of our problems before crossing over to England. The plan is to visit our girls and their partners in England before crossing over to Holland. First of all our GPS needs to be re-programmed because it can't find the satellites. Secondly our VHF is showing antenna failure, and thirdly our hand-held VHF's spare battery pack does not seem to be holding its charge. Not major sounding problems but it is essential to fix them before moving on. Bergen is a lovely town and we parked bang in the city centre with all the conveniences around us. The three boats are frequently filmed and eyed up by the many tourists who stroll by. On *Fereale* we enjoy more privacy than most, owing to her cockpit cover, which we can hide behind. Now that we are on our own we can get into serious navigation mode again. The same counts for the others as all of us need to focus on the next stage, ours being a crossing of some five or six days. We seem to be unable to concentrate on these things, when part of a crowd.

18th August, 2000

Early to rise, but first more job applications. The fish are literally jumping out of the water all around the boat and I am eager to try out my fishing gear. Gordon wisely warned me against it as he had noticed the sewage drain nearby.

Next we moved to the other side of the harbour and, in the pouring rain, filled our tanks with diesel and collected our reprogrammed GPS. An unexpected few hours were spent rewiring the whole lot as the new connector differed from ours. By 4pm we were off at last and on our way to Bekkjarvik, where we did not arrive until ten in the evening, after a disastrous first attempt at fishing and nearly losing our line. From now on we will need to make sure that we drift to deeper rather than shallower water! But at last there is time to relax and both of us are sipping English gin and leftover Russian tonic in the comfort of our cockpit.

To our surprise a harbour master came round expecting payment, not bad though as this is only the second time we have been asked for money since we arrived in Norway. However, he tried to charge us more than the fee I had seen written on the board, something I duly pointed out.

Fisherman At Last

19th August, 2000

Deciding to make the most of what was left of our holiday we stopped halfway through the morning and had another attempt at fishing. Excitedly we hauled up our first couple of mackerel after an incredible two minutes. Our aft deck proved to be an ideal place for an apprentice like myself to have her first attempt at gutting and cleaning. Still feeling a bit bad about having to kill the poor animals, I apologised to every fish whose head was about to be chopped off. During another attempt later on in the day we caught another eight, all within the space of one hour. Loosing at least another four, including some much larger than mackerel. Another nice fat cod would have been good, but we are not complaining. At least my dream has come true and I will be able to give Brenda a couple of mackerel for her birthday. Very tired but happy with life, we arrived in Kopervik by nine in the evening.

20th August, 2000

After a leisurely start *Fereale* was on her way but making a miserable speed of two knots. Having discovered a new hobby, and with Stavanger not far away, we fished until our freezer was full and could take no more. What a life—to catch your own dinner and eat it within half an hour from the comfort of your cockpit whilst under sail. To our surprise we were the first of the three boats to arrive in Vågen harbour, in the centre of the town of Stavanger.

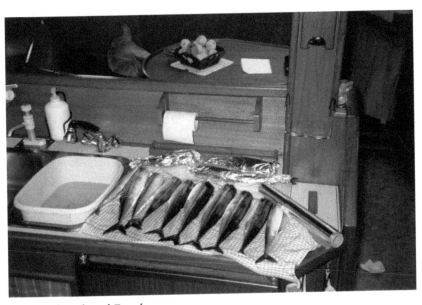

First catch on board Fereale

22nd August, 2000

A few fun days passed, with all of us doing our own thing. Brenda and Alan got their boat ready for a passage to Scotland, whilst Elsbeth and Willem prepared to sail to Holland. We, ourselves, were getting *Fereale* ready for our trip to England. Many letters have gone out to agents over the last week or so regarding work for Gordon. What we had not counted on, however, was that our little Psion could not handle the huge documents that they sent us in return. Our system crashed and we were unable to get it to talk to us from then on. Elsbeth, who had watched our struggle, came to the rescue and together we opened a Hotmail account at the local library. "From there you can access your own account," she said, "and send anything out via Hotmail." It was a system she and many others had been using all along. Once she had shown me how, we were back in business, but the emails that had come in were depressing. All of them were basically telling us that there was no work. Asea Brown Boveri (ABB), the company Gordon had worked for in Holland, was the only one that gave us some hope, but no certainty.

We shall have to see what happens regarding our sail to England, as a deep depression is heading our way from the west of Ireland. Stavanger is hosting an oil festival at the moment and all around the harbour there are tents with live music events and food stalls. Although very noisy it is great fun and all of us are in a party mood.

23rd August, 2000

Even though it is blowing hard today, Willem and Elsbeth have decided to make a trip to the glaciers. As Elsbeth carefully manoeuvred *Spirit of Aeolus* out of their tight berth I could hardly watch and felt sure that something was going to happen. Suddenly commotion, and we watched *Spirit* crash into another boat. A most unfortunate incident in which their gears and bow thrusters failed just at the crucial moment. Some of the people on the other boat were still sleeping at the time and had the shock of their lives. Investigation showed a large crack in the fibreglass hull of the other boat, whose skipper and crew were about to depart for England. Concerned, we watched them leave that same day, something that often happens when skipper and crew are under pressure of time. *Spirit of Aeolus*, with flat batteries and no further damage than its cables, spent the rest of the day surrounded by mechanics.

Parting Company

24th August, 2000

Brenda and Alan were the first to leave our tiny fleet. I desperately wanted to tell them not to go, or at least not yet, as the distance they were to cover, and the unsettled weather, had made me feel uneasy. It was an emotional moment when in the early morning Willem, Elsbeth, Gordon and I, all dressed in waterproofs, said goodbye to Brenda and Alan in the pouring rain. An end had come, to our travelling together.

25th August, 2000

At 2am we were rudely awoken when an unexpected visitor boarded *Fereale*. Sitting on our aft hatch was a young lad, exhausted from running and hardly able to speak. Whilst huffing and puffing and scanning the shore, he told us that he had been chased and that people were trying to kill him. "You are safe now," I said, "so don't worry." But nothing would comfort him and we were pleased when he asked me to call the police, but cautious, also, as most likely this was drug related. Careful not to hand him our mobile, I called the police myself and gave them instructions on how to find us. This scared our young man, who then panicked and ran away to disappear into the crowds ashore. A sad reflection of what hides behind the curtains of our seemingly normal life. For ages I waited for the police to arrive, whose searchlights I could see from the shore. Having forgotten the telephone number of the police I had been given I was unable to call them a second time and gave up waiting after an hour or so.

This time it is our turn to leave Stavanger and head further south, possibly for

Tananger, before making our crossing over to England. Needing shelter from wind and rain, and after an unsuccessful attempt at locating a diesel station, we moored up at the bottom of someone's garden. The space was reserved for another boat, but from there we could scan the area for our diesel station and perhaps inspect the engine room. With a face covered in soot Gordon announced that he had come face to face with a broken exhaust. Although dismayed, it was amazing, really, that the simple repair carried out in Murmansk had held for as long as it had. The owners of the property welcomed us with open arms, allowing us to stay as long as was needed. They were wonderful people, called Laila and Toralv, and we all became good friends. Gordon soon set to work in the filthy conditions of our engine room, taking apart the broken exhaust and finishing the day with a cold shower in our cockpit.

The next few days were spent travelling back and forth to Stavanger by bus, where we found an agent prepared to make a new section of exhaust. In our spare time we visited the library and emailed our family on work-related issues. On one such a day we met Willem and Elsbeth, whom we had thought were well on their way to Holland. They were stranded, they said, in Egersund with serious starter motor problems and had been towed in by the local SAR team. Like us they were waiting for repairs and suggested having a coffee together in town. All of us wondered whereabouts Brenda and Alan were. Somewhere out there in the middle of the North Sea anyway. At least that is what we thought!

28th August, 2000
Our delay was obviously meant to happen as Gordon discovered another two potentially very dangerous electrical problems. It seemed that a couple of original connections had melted through—that of the domestic water pump and diesel transfer pump. Although still in working order, if not discovered they could have caused a fire and major problems at sea, as likely as not at the most inconvenient moments or sea state. I have a strong feeling that someone is watching over us.

31st August, 2000
With our new exhaust in place we moved back to Vågen harbour. Laila and Toralv were sad to see us leave as both of them had enjoyed the excitement of having a Dutch boat at the bottom of their garden. Toralv, who had been

offended by the size of our Norwegian courtesy flag, presented us with a larger one, to which we responded by giving him our Friesian one. We shall miss them and the kindness of all the Norwegian people. It was blowing hard outside and all night we worried about the depressions that were surrounding us. But it had been a good day for Gordon, who had been half promised his job back, together with some agents showing an interest at last.

1st September, 2000
With renewed energy Gordon installed a new motor for our windscreen wipers, another long overdue project and never straightforward. All of this before we left Stavanger for good and headed towards Tananger. Another attempt at fishing on the way rewarded us with eighteen mackerel—our best catch ever. Our celebration, however, ended abruptly when the captain split his head open on the boom. Slightly subdued and with a five-centimetre gash on his crown, we entered Tananger.

2nd September, 2000
Another beautiful day in harbour, sheltered from the wind coming from all directions. It has been difficult to get a reliable five- to six-day forecast, but *Fereale* is prepared and we are ready to go. We need to leave tomorrow if we are to have a favourable wind. At last there was news from Willem and Elsbeth and their email told us that they had arrived safely in Holland. It had been a fast but scary sail apparently, with a near collision in the vicinity of the shipping lanes.

Exhaust Problems, Again

3rd September, 2000

We left Tananger at six o'clock in the morning and for the last time admired the beautiful sunrise before heading out to sea. But barely two hours into our journey our peace was shattered. Nearly overcome by fumes, Gordon came to the cockpit to tell me that our brand-new exhaust had cracked. Not just a little, but totally this time. Still coughing and spluttering from the deadly carbon monoxide fumes in the engine room, he told me that our engine room was black once more. Slowly we turned *Fereale* around and headed back towards Tananger, to reflect on what had happened and get stuck in. Inside my heart is aching from having to watch him go through this pain, of being able to do so little and the worry of what to do next. All I can do is have an attempt at cleaning the engine room and be there as background support. With the knowledge of a potentially long delay we decided to change our plan and head for Holland instead of England when all was well and done. A decision fully supported by our family. Gordon spent the afternoon drawing up sizes and measurements of our exhaust system and a possible different route. Being a Sunday there was little else he could do. Once again my faith in his ability to solve the problem and in our safe completion of the trip never failed. However hard at the time, everything was meant to happen.

4th September, 2000

We travelled by bus to the company that had supplied our new exhaust and who, baffled like us, took full responsibility. We could not have asked for more and left with the promise of a quick turnaround. Deep in his heart Gordon knows that the next section of exhaust is not going to be the final cure, but is hoping that it will take us as far as Holland at least.

7th September, 2000

It took two days to clean our engine room, during which time every spare bit of cloth and paper was utilised. The entire contents came out, including the floors, after which it once more looked respectable, a job we hope never to repeat again. The new exhaust looked very much like the old one did but a bit more flexible. Time to put it to the test. We are in no hurry to sail to Holland anyway as a storm is brewing.

Under engine we set off and motored towards the sea, but by the time a few hours had gone by the storm had reached its full strength. Together with the fishing boats *Fereale* ploughed her way back to the harbour against the wind. All of us were seeking refuge and were pleased not to be out there any longer than necessary. Hearing the wind howl around us every night and knowing that we have a big passage ahead is unsettling us both. Although the exhaust had held *Fereale* kindly pointed out another problem to us, one in need of urgent repair. On our return to harbour I discovered that our forward bunks were soaked in diesel. It seemed that the hose underneath the deck connection that leads to our diesel tank had come away from its fitting. The rough motion at sea had made the diesel spill over the top and run straight into our bedding. Well done, *Fereale*, and thank you, as this would have been impossible to fix whilst at sea, especially in bad weather. This particular diesel tank means a lot to us, as it is the only one out of the three that we can use. The others still have bad Russian diesel in them and can't be cleaned until we are back home.

8th September, 2000

With at least another day in hand I set about washing our clothes and sheets. Using a couple of large buckets, I carried load after load to the shower facilities where I washed and rinsed and got totally soaked in the process. In the meantime Gordon, having found a welder, is having our stainless steel deck fitting lengthened.

Local people often come by and inquire about *Fereale* and her travels. One particular visitor seemed to know all about our trip. He said that he had heard of a Norwegian who had recently sailed through Russia. A Stavanger newspaper apparently had covered the story of André in *Endring*, who had been part of our tiny fleet. His journey had ended in Stavanger, the point from which he had started, having circumnavigated his country and the whole of Scandinavia. Excitedly I rushed to a local telephone kiosk and left a message on his answer machine. It would be wonderful if he could visit us and we could meet up once more. It did not take long before he had returned our call. He was delighted, but also surprised, at finding us still in Norway. Of course he was coming, as being back at work for him was hard. He needed to see us, he said, together with our boat, and make sure that all we had experienced together had not been a dream.

9th September, 2000

Gordon had only just managed to put the fitting back in place when André arrived on his bike. It was great to see him and his company gave us a welcome break. Though, having shaved off his beard we hardly recognised him! He stayed for dinner after which he wished us well and left, quite envious that our trip was not yet over, like his.

At last we received news from Brenda and Alan. On a daily basis I had been emailing them asking for news. It seemed that their first night at sea after leaving Stavanger for Scotland had been a rough one. Force seven, frequent gusts of forty knots and a big running sea had highlighted a serious problem. Their forepeak was leaking badly, a result of hitting the side of the Belomorsk lock in Russia. Not feeling safe to continue their two-hundred-mile passage to Scotland they had decided to return to Norway. From then on they had coast-hopped to Denmark, where the problem was fixed once and for all. They were on their way to Holland, they said, via the Kattegat and the Kiel Canal and wished us well. I don't think somehow that we will meet them in Holland, as both Brenda and Alan are keen to get home.

10th September, 2000

We left Tananger quite unexpectedly, as our Navtex suddenly showed a reasonable five-day forecast. We had to take advantage of it. Slowly the beautiful Norwegian coastline disappeared from the horizon. But this time we couldn't look back as we have to concentrate on what is ahead and settle into a routine.

All four of our sea legs have gone and silently each of us is getting on with our job. The sea is confused and there is a leftover swell coming from the west. We are motor sailing and are still checking our exhaust with frequent trips to the engine room. So far so good, and from our next waypoint onwards our engine will be switched off and only the wind will push us forwards. From then on we will take turns to rest and prepare ourselves for three or four nights at sea, depending on wind strength and direction. Both of us are feeling sick and the heavens have opened up. It looks as if we have been away from the open sea for too long!

Back in Dutch Waters

11th September, 2000

One night has gone by, with a wonderful star-filled sky. I have problems sleeping, but all of that will soon change. Life is certainly full of surprises. When it was time to charge our batteries, nothing happened. They totally refused to accept any charge, which baffled Gordon. Our generator did charge them but at a much slower rate. Why, oh why, should this problem have to show itself now, when we still need to cross the shipping lanes and need the use of our navigation lights and radar? It was not until the next day that Gordon had a surprise find in our engine room. Lying in the bilges was the missing plug; a plug that had got knocked off during our cleaning exercise, and one that he did not know was missing until he found it. He stuck it where it belonged, after which we were back in business. 'A well-deserved beer for the chief engineer' was the entry in his log.

Waking me up from my sleep, Gordon asked for help with reefing our sails and taking down the yankee as a force seven or more was brewing. *Fereale*, feeling more comfortable, nevertheless had a rough night. White-encrusted waves constantly engulfed her, and both of us were feeling sick. Gordon, whose stomach is stronger than mine, has been up for eleven hours, due to a dinner I cooked that did not settle in my stomach. Corned beef hash, something Alan taught me how to cook. He will be getting the blame for this, poor chap.

Holland is getting closer all the time and in about five hours' time we should have reached the shipping lanes north of Terschelling. Unfortunately it will be dark when we cross the lanes, but at least we have radar. It is most important that we get enough sleep, as the wind is still increasing in strength. Writing is hard, as I am constantly up and down adjusting sails or busy navigating. Visibility is poor but both *Fereale* and crew are doing well.

When the time came Gordon actually trusted me to cross the shipping lanes whilst he took a nap on the floor of our saloon, to be near me if needed and to avoid being thrown out of his bunk. Somehow we needed to slow down, as we didn't fancy arriving in the dark. Our timing was perfect and just about at daybreak we turned towards Vlieland's harbour entrance. This is where we met an exodus of boats, catching the early morning tide towards the Waddenzee. It has taken us three days and three nights, which is not bad going for *Fereale*. An incredible feeling overwhelmed us both, once we were safely moored up. The reality that we had sailed four thousand eight hundred miles had finally hit us. It was time to celebrate, but not before calling Mum and family, and not before cleaning the boat, clearing customs and having a good shower. Only then were we able to catch up on some much-needed sleep and splash out on a meal ashore.

It is nice to be back but the reality of having to pay horrendous harbour fees is hitting us hard. We shall have to return to Warmond as soon as possible if our funds are to last, two nights in Vlieland is the most we can afford. Suddenly our freedom seems to have gone and I feel almost scared to confront the busy harbours, locks and waterways. The open sea is beckoning us to return and a Dutch poem springs to mind, one that I translated. It seems to reflect the mood I am in.

14th September, 2000

Slowly we motored out of Vlieland's harbour and raised our sails catching the flood tide to Harlingen. There we will meet my mum and Willem and Elsbeth, who are in the midst of laying up *Spirit of Aeolus* for a refit and paint job. Motorway sailing, I call this, as we keep to starboard of the narrow channels between the sandbanks.

After three hours we arrived in a delightful little harbour with a brand-new clubhouse. The smallest harbour we have ever had to squeeze into. Mum is excited at the prospect of seeing us again and always moulds herself around our plans. She loves being on the boat and travels lighter than any visitor we have ever had. We had a lovely afternoon, entertaining her with our stories and

The Sea
Noises
So familiar
Always different
Mother nature
So beautiful

So Beautiful
The sea
Full of life
And movement
Time and again
Emotion
When I see you

When I See You
I know
This is
Where I belong
You I love the most
Ebb and flow

Ebb and Flow
Like life
Seagulls that fly
Over the waves
Playing with the wind

The Wind
Takes me along
To the sea
Back to nature
Where I find myself
In all my sensitivity

those of Willem and Elsbeth, who joined us for dinner.

15th September, 2000
It's the captain's birthday and it's lovely to have Mum here to celebrate it with us. Gordon just loves to be spoiled, and cards, presents and calls from our children were the order of the day.

It was time to move on, but not before another visit to our engine room. Ever since Petrozavodsk Gordon has had to take daily samples of our diesel, to check for water and dirt at the bottom of our day tank. We are fortunate to have access to the bottom of that tank where he is able to drain off any nasties, only to find more every day after the diesel has been churned up at sea. We are most at risk when our engine has been used at sea. This is when there is no time for the water to settle, owing to the motion of the boat. The draining has to be done when *Fereale* is at rest and water and dirt have settled. It is amazing how our eighty horsepower engine has survived so far without a murmur of complaint. The slightest water in her injectors would be like rat poison to a human being.

Slowly we turn *Fereale* around and squeeze her out of the harbour's narrow exit. The scenery is so different from what we have seen over the last few months and the distances to cover so small. We are on our way to Leeuwarden, the town where I went to school. We have never visited Friesland with *Fereale* before, something we have done with every other boat so far. In Leeuwarden we will pick up my sister, Inge, who will travel with us as far as Warmond. Another reason for going through Friesland is to visit the town of Woudsend, where *Fereale* was built in 1980. There we hope to meet her builder, a man called Mr Kuipers. Everyone in Holland knows his name and we are proud to own one of his ships. Yes, *Fereale* feels a bit like a ship to us, almost more than a boat. Having sailed her himself for five years, I am sure he will be pleased to see her. Perhaps he still has some old drawings... it is worth asking anyway.

One of Gordon's birthday treats is a visit to Franeker, to see the oldest working planetarium in the world. Mum is loving every minute and sits wrapped up in one of our orange fur-lined coats behind the windscreen in our cockpit.

In Franeker we tied up near the centre of town, which is easy to do in the month of September as the quays are reasonably empty. Just as the three of us prepared to leave, Gordon discovered that yet again our engine room was filled with smoke and dangerous fumes. Mum, hiding in a corner, stayed well out of our way. She is good at that and appreciates our tense moments. I don't know whether to laugh or cry but am pleased that we have made it across the North Sea without incident. We must look at the positive side, as we could not be in a better place. Holland after all is a country full of water, boats and plenty of yards to choose from. "It's my birthday," Gordon said; "let's go! Nothing is going to stop me seeing my planetarium." Slightly subdued we soon found the signs leading us into town, determined to have a good time. Mum, quietly following in our wake, did not dare interrupt our train of thought. Before long we arrived at the house where Eise Eisinga used to live. This is where Eise, a fanatical astronomer, built a planetarium in his living room in 1774; a project that took him seven years to complete and which hung from the ceiling of his living room. Made out of wood, the structure was put together with tens of thousands of handmade nails. From there we were able to watch the exact position of the stars and planets and that of the sun and moon. Everything was in working order and even showed the correct time and date, including that of the full eclipse of sun and moon. It was this that Eise wanted to explain to the rest of the world, and the reason for his project.

Next it was time to have lunch and ponder our strategy over a large beer. Mum is thinking that it may be better for her to take the train home. Not bad thinking, as this is not exactly the fun we had planned for her. It is well into the afternoon now and we wonder if the yards will still be open. It looks as if I will need to start hugging the phone, as Gordon has still not conquered the Dutch language. Back in The Hague everyone speaks English, which is not always the case in the little villages up north. Luck was with us as unbelievably there was a yard a few hundred yards away willing to have a look. It is a dangerous problem after all and one that can cost a life. Very carefully we motored the short distance, where Gordon, together with some workmen, decided on two new bellows and a new support. Whilst the men did their engineering bit, Mum packed her bags. It must be no fun being with us when our only thought is how to tackle our problem, but it saddens me to see her go. We are happy, though, with the knowledge that the yard was helping us, and that work will start tomorrow. Together we waved her goodbye on her way to the station, after which I cycled into town and bought as many cloths as I could find to help clean the sooty engine room.

16th September, 2000

"So far I have had to be the judge of things," Gordon said. "Let's see how the professionals have done this time." With a heavily-reduced bank balance we left the yard in the early afternoon. All we want is for these bellows to get us home; once there we can take our time and do things properly like we have always done. Gordon's former boss has told him that he should pay him a visit on his return. It sounds hopeful but nothing is certain yet. Our checks every ten minutes show no sign of any problem, which feels almost too good to be true.

Leeuwarden, the capital of Friesland, is our next port of call. I grew up there in a small village called Tietjerk, just outside the town and bang in the middle of the countryside. At school and with our friends from the surrounding farms we spoke Friesian, but once back home we switched to Dutch. I will never forget catching rides on a horse-drawn milk cart, whose daily route went past our house. I remember the many occasions we were invited by friends from surrounding farms to watch a cow drop her calf, and the fun we had rummaging in haystacks and sailing on the lakes. As we slowly pass the meadows I reflect and smell my youth once more. Mum, in whose thoughts we have been every inch of our five thousand miles, was there to welcome us. She drove from bridge to bridge, leading us into the centre of the town, waving enthusiastically and taking pictures. This is something she has done before in previous times when we sailed over from England, but that was with Dad. Suddenly I miss him and can visualise him standing next to her.

Our aim is to moor up at the Prinsentuin, a park in the centre of town and another trip down memory lane. A memory, that takes us back to when our eldest daughter was born in the hospital opposite, now an old people's home, Gordon came to visit us in hospital, having sailed there. After having moored up the boat directly opposite he walked into the maternity ward still wearing his yellow sailing boots.

A few fun days passed, with us visiting family and family visiting us. Willem and Elsbeth from *Spirit of Aeolus* dropped by and showed us the videos they had taken of our travels through Russia. Even my sister, Inge, was able to see some of it as she had come by train and had joined *Fereale*. I wonder how Gordon and I are going to digest all of the things that have happened to us over the last five months.

19th September, 2000

It is time to move on and do something we have wanted to do for a long time; to make our way to Woudsend, where we can hopefully meet up with *Fereale*'s first owner, designer and builder. Having my sister with us is fun and we love to share our boat life with her. It is pretty shallow everywhere and after getting stuck a few times we near Woudsend. Mr Kuipers, I am sure, will be able to tell us where the best place is to moor up, if indeed he is at home. Talking on our mobile I explained to his secretary the reason for our visit, and she promised he would return our call. Slowly we progressed into the village and were contacted just in time to be given instructions of where to meet.

He was delighted that we had got in touch and was keen to see the boat. Only this very summer, he said, he had wondered where she was. Next he asked me if we were aware of *Fereale*'s background, to which I replied that we knew precious little. One of the reasons for our visit after all was to find out more, and perhaps obtain copies of original drawings. I told him that all we knew was that the third owner had bought her from the government and that the second one had had financial difficulties. He then said that he would rummage through his photo albums and find the pictures relating to the various building stages of *Fereale* and copy them for us. Also that he would look up the many newspaper articles written about her, as *Fereale* had been involved in smuggling ten million guilders' worth of hash! Gordon, my sister and I were dumbfounded. Our precious *Fereale* had not only rounded the North Cape but had also sailed up and down to Morocco.

Quietly we moored up on the designated pontoon with enough time to get tidy before meeting Mr Kuipers. But within five minutes of arriving Gordon discovered that our exhaust had broken for the umpteenth time. We could not possibly continue without his help, but how were we to tell him?

Delighted to see his ship again, Mr Kuipers stepped on board laden with albums and newspaper cuttings, having made time for us in his busy schedule. "My ship," he said, as he stood behind her steering wheel. Down below nothing much had changed, he said, and we could see that he was pleased that *Fereale* was in good hands. "Not a problem," he said, when he heard about the exhaust. "I shall put my men on to it and we shall sort it out once and for all."

In the short time he spent with us he explained how, unbeknownst to him, he had sold his *Violet Victory* (now *Fereale*) to a drug dealer. Customs, whose boats he maintains in his yard, had told him that the boat he used to own had been arrested. After a few phone calls to the yard and instructions to his men Mr Kuipers left, leaving us to read about it ourselves, having given us all there was on the subject. As we approached the yard our boat suddenly felt different, if only for a little while. In the evening, having had more time to reflect, we smiled as suddenly our beloved *Fereale* had become infamous.

The hash baron, Gerrit van der M, aged forty-five, did not count his money, but weighed it. After every successful drugs delivery he would drive as fast as he could in his unobtrusive car to his expensive villa in Friesland. There he weighed his money on ordinary kitchen scales, after which he would bury it in his garden, the safes in his house being too small. But early in June 1988 his luck ran out and *Violet Victory* was arrested after a dramatic chase on the IJsselmeer. The chase came to an end in front of the closed locks of Stavoren, where the police discovered nearly two thousand kilos of hash on board. A few days later another one of Gerrit's yachts was arrested carrying nearly sixteen hundred kilos, and after that two more of his yachts were impounded. A total of ten thousand kilos of hash had been smuggled into Holland since 1983, with a street value of thirty million guilders. In the five years that Gerrit owned *Violet Victory* (*Fereale*), she had made many trips up and down to Morocco, which brought in more money than Gerrit was able to spend. He gave thousands of guilders away to the church and to children collecting for charity. They were actions that did not go unnoticed for a man out of work and claiming benefits. In June 1988, Gerrit, together with eleven members of his gang, were arrested and put in jail. *Violet Victory* spent five years in chains before being released and sold by the government. Gerrit claimed that during his time in prison he saw people smoking more hash than he could have ever smuggled into Holland.

Fereale received lots of attention from the yard and her problems were solved once and for all. The engineer in charge had helped build her in the first place. We were very grateful and, who knows, *Fereale* had waited for this very occasion.

Our journey wouldn't be completed until we were safe and well in Warmond, and bemused we cast our lines. On to Lemmer we went, then Monnikendam and Haarlem.

25th September, 2000
On 25th September we reached the Kagerplassen and were home, having been away for five months. Our harbour master and his wife were there to welcome us, and also Reinier, our ever-loyal friend. We shall have to get used to not being on the move anymore and face the reality of earning a living.

*

A year has gone by and it has taken me this long to put our experiences on paper. I surprised myself that it took as long as it did, but could not stop until it was finished in my own way and time. Only now can I move on and be part of a future plan.

Epilogue
by Gordon

Yes, I did enjoy the trip, and fixing things along the way is all part of the cruising life. I may have had more than my fair share of it, but no boat has been exempt. I feel that I have served my apprenticeship to long time cruising now, and in the process have learnt a lot about the boat and myself.

Emotionally I can divide the trip into three phases. First there was the Baltic section, when we were still at the start of our adventure and full of excitement and anticipation. The mechanical problems we had did not feel too bad apart from one potential showstopper in Mariehamn. There was frustration in trying to solve them, but no underlying fear.

The second emotional period was through Russia, where the pressure was on to get *Fereale* safely through. The prospect of being stuck for the winter in Arctic Russia terrified me. To leave the boat behind was equally frightening, since it would have meant leaving our home. It was on this leg that I lost weight. We had business visas, to cover our scheduled month in the country, which we extended to a six-week stay. Not long enough if our problems had kept us in Murmansk. Once inside Russia it proved impossible for André to have the visa of his crew extended. Having only just arrived in Murmansk, he was forced to leave the same day in spite of dubious steering gear. I would therefore suggest to anybody wanting to do the same that they should allow for as much contingency as possible beyond the departure date of your scheduled stay in Russia.

The third period, after reaching Norway, was sheer heaven. The crises had past and we were on our way home. The scenery was stunning and if our

185

schedule had slipped it would not have worried us; in fact, we would have welcomed it. We went all the way to the south without any problems. It was not until we tried to leave Stavanger for the UK that the problem with our exhaust reared its head again. The enforced week's delay was really rather welcome—we did not want to leave. Our exhaust was finally fixed in Holland, when the back end of the pipe was clamped to stop vibration, and the front fitted with a proper expansion joint where it is attached to the engine.

Apart from the magnificent sights we have seen, one of the highlights must be the number of wonderful people we met along the way, both in the fleet and ashore. We made some good friends and feel enriched by the experience. Having been back in the office environment for more than a year now, I am not sure whether I have settled. Our next target is to see when we can go cruising for longer than a mere six months. In 2006 we hope to do just that, and return to Scandinavia with more time on our hands. Our horizon seems unlimited.

Useful Information

Provisioning

Stocking up for a long voyage always requires a lot of thinking and planning in advance. As soon as the decision was made to sail through Russia, I started reading Lin Pardey's book *The Care and Feeding of Sailing Crew*. Anything appropriate to our situation I wrote down in a little book called 'Irene's Bible'.

To minimise large amounts of bags and bottles I bought 5-litre jerry cans, in which I put a variety of dried foods and cleaning products. All of the jerry cans stowed nicely inside *Fereale*'s belly and proved to be a great success.

Around Sweden and Finland most things were available, but once we ventured beyond St Petersburg it was different. Let's say there was no time to shop anyway. If I knew then what I know now, we would have carried a bread maker on board. I was prepared to make bread by hand, but somehow never managed to find the time.

In some ways our journey was treated more as an expedition. Our main aim was to be self-sufficient for one month whilst in Russia. On our way through the Baltic we shopped normally, and it was not until Russia that we delved into our food supply. In St Petersburg we managed to find a supermarket, after which we did not shop for food till Belomorsk. Next came Murmansk, where people from the local sailing club provided us with a warm welcome and much needed assistance.

On board *Fereale* we cook on propane, which is stored in a pair of 10 kg cylinders. We set out with two full bottles, had one refilled in St Petersburg and arrived back in Holland with half a cylinder of gas left. This is an average rate of consumption for *Fereale*. In St Petersburg they grumbled about the incompatible fittings when asked to refill, but relented when Gordon fitted a nozzle and a length of orange gas hose for them.

Propane is preferable to butane in a cold climate as it vaporises better. Some people had the little blue Camping Gas bottles but they had to carry a large number as they are not readily available everywhere.

The availability of engine spares inside Russia was basic. For instance, we bought a new starter battery at Petrozavodsk, but any specialised spares would have had to be flown in. The exhaust was welded in Murmansk at a reasonable cost, but our major fear was that of getting stuck in Russia waiting for spares and, in the worst-case scenario, getting into visa problems and having to leave our boat behind. Luckily, we were well equipped with most things, but inevitably, with hindsight, we would have taken further spares. These additions are included below.

Along with supplies for Gordon, myself and our guests, to show our appreciation to others who helped us along the way, we carried small gifts on board—sufficient to say thank you, and far less embarrassing than money. Most of these I bought at our local tourist shop.

One way or another the shelves on board *Fereale* have never been empty.

The following lists give a rough idea of what we stocked up on before we set sail.

Galley Basics

- *Dried pasta*
- *Rice*
- *Instant mash potato*
- *Flour and yeast*
- *Kidney beans*
- *Baked beans*
- *Porridge*
- *Rye crackers*
- *Cup-a-Soups*
- *Large tins of soup (for emergencies only)*

- *Tomato purée*
- *Beef, chicken, vegetable and fish stock cubes (in thick glass jar with clamp-on top)*
- *Olive oil*
- *Margarine*
- *Salt (in airtight container)*
- *Tinfoil*
- *Cling film*
- *Matches (out of their packets in airtight container)*

Meat & Fish (all tinned)
- Spam
- Corned beef
- Meatballs
- Mince
- Chicken
- Pâté
- Steak and kidney pies
- Tuna
- Frozen meat (from our tiny freezer, did not get touched until Russia)

Fruit & Veg (all tinned)
- Tomatoes
- Peas
- Mushrooms
- Carrots
- Sweet corn
- Fruit

Spices & Sauces
- Parmesan cheese (in airtight container)
- Various spices
- Dried pasta sauces
- Mixed spices for rice (e.g. nasi goreng)
- Marmite
- Mayonnaise
- Tomato ketchup

Sweet
- Sugar
- Jam
- Peanut butter
- Honey
- Chocolate bars
- Raisins (for energy)

Drinks
- Coffee
- Coffee-Mate
- Teabags
- Dried milk (in large screw-top container)
- Cocoa powder
- Karvan (concentrated blackcurrant juice)
- Wine
- Beer

Toiletries & Cleaning
- Toilet rolls
- Toothpaste
- Shampoo
- Wet wipes
- Antibacterial wipes
- Laundry powder
- Washing up liquid
- Bin bags

Medicine Cabinet
- Mosquito coils
- Soda powder (in large screw-top container, most useful for infections)
- Stugeron
- First-aid box with prescription drugs, including their prescriptions, and a sterile kit for stitching up wounds

Spares
- *Dutch flag*
- *Windvane for the Aries*
- *Electric plate for cooking (in case we ran out of gas)*
- *Pressure cooker*
- *Light bulbs*
- *Night lights*
- *Fan belts*
- *Engine hoses*
- *Lubricating oil*
- *Fuel filter elements*
- *Drinking water pump*
- *Engine control cables*
- *Starter motor*
- *Rigging wire and Sta-Lok connectors*
- *Batteries*
- *Film rolls*
- *Disposable cameras*

Gifts
- *Face flannels with windmill designs and little soaps in the shape of Dutch clogs*
- *Tea towels with typical Dutch designs*
- *Bags of typical Dutch sweets*
- *Packets of English tea*
- *Packets of Smarties*
- *Bags of toffees*
- *Bags of chocolates*
- *T-shirts*

Finance

From *The Care and Feeding of Sailing Crew* I even picked up hints on the financial side of things, like keeping small notes rather than large ones. It is awkward when you go shopping if you only carry large denomination notes, as most people are not likely to be in a position to give you back lots of change.

We took with us a small quantity of local currency for each country we were visiting, roughly equivalent to £50, to cover any immediate expenses upon arrival. In addition, we carried cash in US dollars, as we were unsure of the availability of cash machines in Russia. For security the cash was discreetly hidden about the boat.

We didn't keep particularly good records of expenditure and therefore had to make intelligent guesses based on our bank statements, together with our credit card receipts. The approximate costs are listed below, including rally fees.

Charts	£1,500
Fuel	£1,500
Food, drink and entertainment	£3,000
Harbour dues	£400
Repairs and maintenance	£750
Expenses incurred in Russia	£1,600
TOTAL	*£8,750*

The cost of charts might seem extravagant, until you realise that from the White Sea to Stavanger alone requires thirty-five Admiralty charts at a scale of 1/200,000. To get a better scale we recommend the use of Scandinavian charts where possible. When you add an Admiralty Pilot and five volumes of Norwegian Pilots, costs mount up rapidly. Crossing an ocean must be much cheaper than coast hopping!

Documentation

Quite apart from making the boat seaworthy there is a lot more that goes into the planning of such a trip than is listed below. The following list of documentation that should be carried might give some idea.

- National registration of the vessel (several boats had only Small Ships Registration (SSR), but we have always felt more confident with Full Ships Registration)
- Evidence of VAT payment
- Proof of ownership
- Boat insurance documents, including legal insurance
- Ships marine radio licence
- Travel and health insurance, including medical evacuation
- ICC (International Certificate of Competence), needed for some countries en route

It has to be remembered that the skipper is responsible for his crew and will need to make certain that they have insured themselves against medical emergencies including evacuation.

Skipper and crew need to have passports, valid twelve months beyond their intended stay in Russia. Boat documents must be valid for at least six months beyond the date of the intended visit.

To obtain a private visa for Russia requires an invitation from an approved authority, in our case this was organised by the CA—our invitation is shown on page vii.

Invaluable Books

The main sources of information and guidance came from paper charts, pilot books and technical manuals. Here are some of the most important:

- *Boatowners' Mechanical and Electrical Manual* by Nigel Calder (published by Adlard Coles). This book was able to guide us to solutions of the numerous mini crises of a technical nature. When *Endring* had problems with their steering system the book contained detailed sketches so we could go straight to a solution.
- *The Ship Captain's Medical Guide* (published by HMSO). Fortunately, not used much but it was reassuring to have it on the bookshelf.
- *Hollandia's Tien Talen Scheepswoordenboek* (published by Hollandia). This is a ten-language glossary of yachting terms and boat equipment and pretty handy when dealing with mechanics in a foreign port.
- *The Cruising Almanac* (published by the Cruising Association). This gives details of ports, radio channels, weather forecasts and formalities for yachtsmen for the area from Bergen to Gibraltar. To be honest, it is the reason we joined the Cruising Association all those years ago. Unfortunately, it does not cover the Baltic Sea east of Denmark, Inland Russia or Northern Norway. Separate references were used in these areas.
- *The Baltic Sea* by the RCC Pilotage Foundation (published Imray). Useful but out of date since its publication in 1992.
- *Euro Regs for Inland Waterways* (published by the RYA). One needs to be able to demonstrate to officialdom that there is a copy on board.
- Miscellaneous inland charts were loaned to us by the Russians and returned

to them when we left.

- *Southern Barents Sea and Beloye More Pilot* (published by the UK Hydrographic Office). Impressive to have on the bookshelf but we did not use it much. It is a bit dry and also scary to read.
- *Norway Pilot Volume 1, NP56* (published by the UK Hydrographic Office). If needed this would have taken us along the south coast of Norway as far as Sweden.
- *Den Norske Los* (Norwegian pilot books), volumes 3a, 3b, 4, 5 and 6, from Bergen to the Russian Border (published by the Norges Sjøkartverk). These provide wonderful detail of the Norwegian coast including a lot of data, tidal information, harbour plans, etc., but the most attractive feature has got to be the aerial photographs. These all seem to have been taken in perfect weather and make you want to visit again and again. All of them are written in Norwegian but somehow we managed to decipher them. They were expensive so we did not buy the final volumes to take us further south.
- *Norwegian Cruising Guide* by Mark Brackenbury (published by Stanford Maritime). This is a slim volume but guided us from Bergen to Stavanger.

For more general interest we carried:

- *Whales, Dolphins and Porpoises* (published by Dorling Kindersley). This proved a popular book for identifying some of our travelling companions.
- *Times Atlas of the World* (published by Times Books). Not really needed for navigation but invaluable when planning long trips. However, it is a bit bulky and heavy.

Addresses &
Contact Information

Cruising Association
CA House
1 Northey Street
Limehouse Basin
London
E14 8BT
(England, UK)
Tel: +44 (0)20 7537 2828
Email: office@cruising.org.uk
Web: www.theCA.org.uk

UK Visa and Passport Service
Web: www.gov.uk/browse/abroad/travel-abroad

Embassy of the Russian Federation, consular section
5 Kensington Palace Gardens
London
W8 4QS
(England, UK)
(Entrance from Bayswater Road)
Tel: +44 (0) 203 668 7474
Email: info@rusemb.org.uk
Web: www.rusemb.org.uk/consular

British Embassy in Moscow, Russia
Smolenskaya Naberezhnaya 10
Moscow 121099
Russia
Tel: +7 495 956 7200
Fax: +7 495 956 7201
Email: ukinrussia@fco.gov.uk
Web: www.gov.uk/government/world/russia

Mr Vladimir Ivankiv
St Petersburg 194354
Russia
Home Tel: +7 812 510 7602
Mobile: +7 921 932 5831
Email: vladimir@sailrussia.spb.ru

Additional information (St Petersburg) Marina Ivankiv
Tel: +7 921 928 2606
Email: ivankiv@yahoo.com

CPSIA information can be obtained
at www.ICGtesting.com
Printed in the USA
LVHW070302021020
667693LV00017BA/1751

9 781916 387317